The Novels of
WALDO
FRANK

WALDO FRANK, 1921

(Photo by Alfred Stieglitz, used by permission of Georgia O'Keeffe.)

The Novels of
WALDO
FRANK

by WILLIAM BITTNER

Philadelphia
University of Pennsylvania Press

TO

WILLIAM R. NORTH

'MYN OWENE MAYSTER DERE'

Preface

IT WAS ROBERT E. SPILLER WHO FIRST SUGGESTED TO ME THAT an inquiry into the work of Waldo Frank might contribute to our understanding of the literary history of the United States. In deciding whether the investigation was worth making I consulted two sets of materials: the works of Waldo Frank and critical studies of him, ranging from book reviews and comments in literary histories to several long articles and two books. After having read through his works once I concluded that Frank was certainly interesting enough for investigation, and I perceived a continual development that seemed to center on his fiction. He was "worth doing"; had he been "done?"

The only previous book-length study of Frank's work (the other book is a symposium), Gorham Munson's *Waldo Frank: A Study*, comes to the same conclusion that I had about his continual development—but it was published in 1923. Since Waldo Frank has continued that development more than thirty years longer and has apparently not stopped yet, Mr. Munson's study did not deter me from the job, although it helped me find my way. A similar incompleteness made all the other studies inadequate: the latest one that treats Frank's work as a whole was published in 1941; the reviews are concerned with only one book, and not the development. Therefore, although they helped me decide to do the work, and I considered the judgments of each, previous studies could not shape or guide this study, which is intended to take great advantage of the perspective only time would provide.

Having decided that Waldo Frank deserves a book, I returned to his works, and in addition turned to two more large sources of information: documents relating to his life and works and the memories of people who know him and his work, including Mr. Frank's own memories. When I had enough information that I could begin organizing it, I became convinced that his fiction is the key to Waldo Frank—to his writings and to his own development. I became equally convinced that not one but several studies need to be made of Waldo Frank, and that my study, in order to be effectively unified, should not consider him as a literary influence, critic, philosopher per se, nor should I discuss his reception abroad. The story of Waldo Frank and Latin America could make a long book by itself; some miscellaneous writings from one of his visits there have already made one book, *Waldo Frank in America Hispana*, edited by M. J. Benardete and published by the Instituto de las Españas en los Estados Unidos.

I decided therefore to discuss only the novels of Waldo Frank and the circumstances surrounding their creation, except insofar as his other writings and relationships are part of those circumstances. This is not a trivial task. Not only are his novels productive of more controversy—indeed critical confusion—than any of his other works, or almost anybody else's, but since they are central to his career, a study of Waldo Frank's novels could provide point of view for further study of him and his work. I wanted to build a foundation that others could rely on, and so I chose as critical method a modification of the method of John Livingston Lowes, who brought to play both historical evidence and semantic analysis.

I have tried to discover and select facts about Waldo Frank, his materials, and the result of the contact between these two things that would illuminate the artist, the creative process, and the work of art. Although I frequently record my impressions as provocations to the reader, and come to some conclusions about what Waldo Frank has tried to do in his novels and how well he succeeded in doing it, each person must decide for himself if it was worth doing and if the result is of permanent significance by reading the novels themselves. Judgments of taste always are made by the discriminating reader for himself; the function of the critic is to air the room, clean the cups, and pour out a fair sample of the wine. I have tried to do that without cheating the vintner or the taster.

No "subject" could have been more cooperative and more trusting throughout this long investigation than was Waldo Frank. He withheld no document; indeed, he opened his files to me and walked away. When the suggestion was made, he deposited in the Rare Book and Manuscript Collection of the University of Pennsylvania all his manuscripts and letters save those that were necessary for current work. Notebooks, kept from 1909 to the present, which in addition to being records of plans and works in progress increasingly became diaries, recording the state of Mr. Frank's mind, were not deposited in the Library, for they are exceedingly personal records, enumerating far more about Waldo Frank's life than most people care to remember about their own lives; yet Mr. Frank turned them over to me without a reservation. Finally, he subjected himself to numberless inquisitorials, without evading a single question; let me watch him as a biologist watches a specimen, without wriggling under the magnifying glass; and treated me as a friend, without attempting to influence my judgments or direct my inquiry. Therefore any error of fact or judgment is not his but mine; and any truth herein would have been much harder to come by and to prove had he and many others not given me the information which they gave so freely.

Far more helpful than any of the published studies were the comments, suggestions, and information given me by many busy people who took time to discuss with me the life and work of Waldo Frank. Among these were Gorham Munson, Lewis Mumford, Catharine and Roderick Seidenberg, Harold Clurman, Dorothy Oko, M. J. Benardete, Dorothy Norman, Oscar Cargill, Mr. and Mrs. Leo Ornstein, and Stella Bloch Hanau and her brother, Eugene Bloch. A long perspective was made available to me through Waldo Frank's brother and sister, Mr. Joseph J. Frank and Mrs. Morton Goldsmith. Jerome Kloucek allowed me access to his enormous bibliography of Waldo Frank. I have received great aid from the use of numerous libraries, so many that I can single out for special mention only Dr. Charles David, of the University of Pennsylvania Library, who not only allowed me a free hand in arranging the Waldo Frank papers but even paid me to do it, and Mr. Thomas R. Adams, then Curator of the Rare Book Collection, and Mrs. Neda M. Westlake, his assistant. As well as Dr. Spiller, Dr. E. Sculley Bradley of the University of Pennsylvania, and Christopher Foster of Cambridge University read each draft of the manuscript and made many helpful suggestions. Very special thanks are owing to Mrs. Elva dePue Matthews, who not only corrected many errors of fact and judgment, but, rarest of critics, told me where I was right, in no uncertain terms!

W. B.

Contents

Contents

The Novels of
WALDO
FRANK

1

A Perspective on
Waldo Frank

THE CAREER OF WALDO FRANK HAS BEEN A MATTER OF CRITICAL
confusion for four decades. During that time his work has run
parallel from time to time with a number of popular interests
but has eventually turned away from almost every one, following its own inexorable course. He has won and lost a variety
of audiences. In 1919 his *Our America* gained him national
respect as a social critic. Through the five years following, his
"lyric" novels won him international renown. *Virgin Spain* and
America Hispana made him a figure of great celebrity in Spanish-
speaking countries. His longer novels of the mid-thirties won
approval from left-wing readers, but what they were really ap-
plauding was his participation in the revolutionary movement.

He eventually alienated every group that admired him for
reasons only incidental to what he really was: the liberals, the
esthetes, the radicals, the Jews; and he never appealed to the
conservatives, the academicians, and the blurb-writing reviewers.
He made a significant contribution in almost every area open
to the intellectual and artistic American, and almost wilfully
threw away the reputation such deeds brought him. By the
1950's he was virtually unknown to the younger generation, the

group that, decade after decade, had been the audience he could count on.

The turning point seems, however, to have been passed. *Bridgehead*, his recent book on Israel, succeeded in spite of violent disapproval from Zionist quarters, because its appeal is general and not to a specific group. It is the main current of his thought that readers of that book are interested in, not the tributary of a common cause. Earlier readers simply objected to the same things he objected to; approving readers of *Bridgehead* find in it a vision that seems akin to what they are seeking. The forthcoming publication of *The Rediscovery of Man* (the culmination of his cultural-religious philosophy) may turn his work and the literary interests of his country, so long divergent, clearly into the same channel.

The basis of all of Frank's writing is his sense of the unity of all things: this unifying force in the multiverse he calls God; not a being or an object, but an action, expressing itself through its parts, among which are persons, peoples, and the total dynamics of creation. Philosophically, he fits in with Emerson, Thoreau, and Whitman. He continues Emerson's concept of the Whole Man and Whitman's "I" who is both Walt Whitman and mankind. To Frank, achievement of the self, becoming a Person, conscious of oneself as a part of the Whole, involves recognition of being partial—existing only in relation to all other persons and all other things—and at the same time involves recognition of God—not fragmented, but entire—within oneself. The Person aware of God within him does not live "in terms of the part as if it were the whole," but "in terms of the Whole expressed through its parts." If God is within the Person, God can be within the People, and achievement of harmony in a society—harmony within itself and harmony with other societies —involves the same awareness on the part of a people.

This concept has important sociological ramifications. Frank believes that we are living in an order, disintegrating since the

Renaissance, centered on faith in human reason. It is homo-
centric, and becomes reduced to egoism. When each ego, be
it of individual, group, nation, church, considers itself as a
noun, a thing, it strives against the others for power. Frank
proposes that each of these consider itself a verb. He says, to
quote from *The Re-Discovery of America*, "Suppose our possible group defines as the one substantive, the one noun, the
Whole of life. Then all that functions wholly within it—expresses the Whole—will be a focus of action or a verb. *The
Whole acting in a certain way will be you or I; and this intrinsic
harmony of our acts, relating us to the Whole, will join us into
a group. . . .*

"The archaic 'entities'—church, state, God, person, truth,
knowledge, thought, time, space, substance, become correlatives.
They are all actions and foci of action (science at last in this
is corroborating metaphysics): actions in the Whole which, in
so far as consciousness inspirits and informs them, become actions of the Whole. Endow the group's imagination with these
verbs, as profoundly as the old delusive nouns have been in-
doctrinated in us, and the magic is there, the cause of chaos
gone."

Frank's rejection of the individual as an entity, "concrete and
discrete, 'souls' absolute and probably eternal, moving along
irreversible time in a groove where they encounter entities of
the same sort," as he puts it in *Re-Discovery*, results in his having an unconventional attitude toward the characters with whom
he peoples his novels, but does not put him outside the traditions of the modern novel. In his later fiction, Frank has been
engaged in demonstrating the analogy between a healthy society
—a People—and a whole Person. In this too, he has been unconventional. Yet the problem of the person in an egocentric
society is the concern of most of today's younger writers and
even some of the writers of best-sellers.

Waldo Frank's progress toward a program for man in the age of the atom, automation, and the utter conquest of nature, developed in his novels. In the 1920's he demonstrated the concept of the Person in the works he calls the lyric novels; the exposition on this theme came at the end of the decade in *Re-Discovery*. In the 1930's his symphonic novels treated the development of society alongside that of the person; an idea he explained in *Chart for Rough Waters* and *The Jew in Our Day*. In the 1940's he tried out several techniques for expressing the person and society together, as a unity; and *Birth of a World* shows one such occurrence in history. *The Rediscovery of Man* is the accumulated philosophy of his career, but it was demonstrated and tried out first in the fictional *Not Heaven*.

Just as with the classic American writers of the Nineteenth Century, Frank's work has been applauded more outside his own country than in. Few Americans have been as close to modern French literature as he, and in the twenties his work had a great success in France, the effect of which has not worn off. In Russia, where his cultural studies have never been published because the regime would not permit it, his novels received high praise. To Latin America he is the personification of the American dream.

Not since the years immediately following the first world war, before the configuration of disillusionment had appeared to dominate the fiction of the years between the wars, has Frank been considered a leader in the art of the novel. This era, however, dominated by Fitzgerald, Hemingway, Faulkner, has passed. The effect of these writers on the craft certainly continues; but their philosophy of the novel is obsolete. It is certainly significant that although Vance Bourjaily's first novel won notice as the best imitation Hemingway to come out of the second world war, his second should so closely parallel the first half of Frank's *The Death and Birth of David Markand*.

Norman Mailer, who began with an almost exclusively political point of view, has begun to delve, like Frank, into the psychology of society. The quest for self is the theme of the day; and since that has been Frank's theme, an audience may at last be ready to judge him.

2

The Island in
Manhattan

NOW AS IN THE 1880's, THE UPPER WEST SIDE OF MANHATTAN
Island is a place of rows of brownstone houses. The brownstone
ranks are broken now by tall apartment houses, or are battered
relics in streets where Puerto Rican children play, but then the
brown stoops and façades were sharply textured and new. Like
a display of worsteds in a tailor's window, each a trifle different
from the next, but none standing out, they lined the numbered
cross streets from Columbus Circle almost to Columbia University. Then as now, the choice streets were those along the two
parks, and Columbus Avenue, where the elevated railway show-
ered soot and noise, was the least desirable. It was in the economic center of this island of the middle class that Julius J.
Frank bought his four-story brownstone.

Julius J. Frank, the father of Waldo Frank, was born in New
York City on March 3, 1852, the son of a German Jewish immigrant. By the time he bought his Upper West Side house,
he was a successful lawyer with an office in Wall Street. A man
of high ideals, he was a Jeffersonian Democrat and a member
of the Committee of Seventy, a reform organization opposed to
Tammany. Although he abandoned Jewish ritual life, he retained
some contact with religion through membership in the Society

for Ethical Culture. He frequently visited Europe, spoke French
and German, and was acquainted with the classics. For all the
liberalism of his politics, religion, and education, however, he
was unbending in his dignity, and he both expected and respected the same dignity in others.

Waldo Frank's mother, Helene Rosenberg Frank, came from
the Alabama branch of a family of international business people.
During the Civil War, her father had been a blockade runner,
but before the end of the fighting he moved his family through
the lines, and in Reconstruction times he established the Standard Varnish Company in New York City. The Rosenbergs were
more pretentious, more cultivated, and less idealistic than Julius
Frank. Although undoubtedly of Jewish origin, they carried on
few of the traditions, but modelled their behavior after that of
Southern society, always, however, with a European accent.
Mrs. Frank's mother spoke German by preference, and since
she lived with the Franks and was something of a tyrant, both
English and German were the household languages during
Waldo Frank's childhood. The universal enthusiasm of the
Rosenberg family was music. One of the Rosenberg uncles
was in the practice of hiring three professionals—a first violin,
viola, and 'cello, to play quartets with him. The fact that he,
the man who paid, was willing to play second fiddle shows an
artistic integrity unusual among amateurs. Mrs. Frank was, according to the memory of her family, an excellent singer, and
might in different circumstances have become a professional.

The Frank household, typical of the second generation German Jewish middle class, was secure and comfortable, and cere-
monious in its behavior. Mr. Frank was somewhat pompous,
and Mrs. Frank's mother required a personal maid in addition
to the normal complement of servants. The house on Seventy-
eighth Street was surrounded by miles of similar houses, and the
families in them differed as little as the houses themselves. The
children could play in Central Park and only occasionally, in

that vast expanse, come across the poor, who had to walk all
the way from the banks of the East River. They could play in
Riverside Park without ever seeing the "dead end kids" from
San Juan Hill. The Upper West Side was a stable world and
a uniform world. The only squalor one saw was from the
window of an elevated train; the only grandeur, the mansions
along Riverside Drive. During the heat of the summer, the
brownstone houses were closed, sheets were spread over the fur-
niture, and the women and children went off to a summer
resort or, occasionally, to Europe. During the summer of 1889
the Franks were at Long Branch, New Jersey, and it was there,
on August 25, that Waldo Frank was born. In the early fall
they returned to New York, making Waldo a New Yorker in
all but birth.

For all of the uniformity and smugness of the Upper West Side
in its middle class glory, it provided solidarity for the class whose
children contributed more than any other group of Americans
to the intellectual history of our time. This comfortable class
is dispersed now to the suburbs where they have lost their
solidarity through conforming with other uniformities, and
their vitality is diffused into commuting and community triv-
ialities. But before the cost of Manhattan land, taxes, and
servants went beyond the means of this group, they made an
intellectual climate that must have been good to grow up in.

Although the artistic heritage of his mother may have been
a greater influence on Waldo than any characteristic of his
father's, but for his father's understanding and tolerance, he
could not have devoted his life to writing as he did. There was
hardly a thing that father and son agreed on in religion, politics,
or art, and Waldo was always impatient to take on tasks his
father thought he was not ready for. Julius Frank seems to have
been a man of very great patience tempered with firm adherence
to what he considered right, and he made remarkable compro-
mises.

It was undoubtedly some help that Waldo was not the only child. There were two girls, Edna, who died during Waldo's youth, and Enid, and an older boy, Joseph. The two boys shared a large room on the top floor of the house, and Joseph Frank recalls many amusing incidents that illustrate Waldo's rebelliousness against the stern decorum of his father and the smug practicality of their parents' world. "He once actually ran away from home," Mr. Frank told me when I interviewed him in 1953. "Sat on a park bench and was persuaded by a stranger to return for his mother's sake. He was a great tease, and his temper was high. He hurled an iron firetong and later a hairbrush at me, almost cracking my nose with the latter."

At school, Waldo Frank was a brilliant, although disconcerting, pupil. Roderick Seidenberg, a year younger, remembers an oratory contest in 1905 which Frank won with an exciting and almost spellbinding speech on Walt Whitman, "although," Mr. Seidenberg relates, "I doubt if any of the students or faculty had heard of Walt Whitman before Waldo told us about him." In his last year at De Witt Clinton High School, Frank refused to go to English class, claiming that there was nothing being offered there that he did not know already. Finally the principal decided that Waldo's argument probably had some justice to it, and therefore no disciplinary action would be taken if he returned to class. Otherwise, he would fail the course. In spite of being offered this face-saving escape from what must have been an act of impulse, Waldo stood by his principle, and Julius Frank accepted his doing so. He did not graduate from De Witt Clinton because of the missing credit in English.

The St. Agnes Branch of the New York Public Library, a few blocks away from the house on Seventy-eighth Street, probably provided Waldo with a more significant part of his early education than did the high school. At any rate, by the time of his last year in high school his regular use of the library had led him to books that were to have profound effect on his life. Beginning with the chance borrowing of *Resurrection*, he read all the Tolstoy he could find. Thoreau was an early influence on him; so much so that by the time he took William Lyon Phelps's course in American Literature at Yale, he had begun to react against Thoreau, and the paper he wrote on *Walden* is sharply critical. In 1906 he read Robert Hunter's *Poverty*, and with his curiosity aroused by this and similar works on social injustice, he took walks through other parts of the city, getting to know the slums and to observe their inhabitants. His political and religious ideas had moved from the moralistic attitudes of his father to the revolutionary. "About 1901," Joseph Frank reports, "he began to show ideas of faith in his individuality by announcing a new 'Waldensian' religion of which he was going to be the prophet. He nearly drove me wild with his nonsense on a European trip we took together."

The "Waldensian" religion that so irritated Waldo Frank's brother was probably brought on by the first insight of the concept of the Person. In a letter written to me on December 11, 1952, he said:

> Instead of an idea or concept [to explain the Person] let me relate to you a little incident which I have never forgotten because I think it suggests the Leitmotif of my entire career. When I was a child, perhaps ten, I returned home one late afternoon in the snow. . . . At the foot of the stoop of our house I saw a small black cat—in the snow. I thought: What if I were the cat? And then came a blinding revelation: If I were the cat, *nothing would be different*. At the time, of course, I could not analyze or intellectualize this conviction of an Identity [between parts of the Whole], as I could now: of the paradox of unity in diversity.

How clearly he saw that concept then is difficult to say, but from the same consciousness that considered this experience a revelation emerged eventually a disbelief in the existence of isolated individuals. Waldo Frank eschews the word *individual*, using in place of it *person*, when he is referring to what he calls the "potential person," and capitalizing *Person* when referring to one aware of his place in the cosmos and the presence of the cosmic in him. No person, he believes, has existence outside the collective conscious, and he calls that collective conscious God. "God is within you," he says, and at the age of fourteen, having already decided that he would become a writer, he put in his notebook, "Every book I write shall be a proof of God."

It is not unusual for a fourteen-year-old to decide that he is going to be a writer, and for him to be keeping a notebook and writing poems and stories. Especially was it not surprising since in the Frank family it was the practice for the children not to buy presents for their parents' birthdays; the present had to be something the child had made. Family concerts were given, and sometimes plays that Waldo wrote. Copies of a number of poems, essays, and stories written as birthday presents for his father are preserved in the Waldo Frank papers, now in the Rare Book and Manuscript Collection of the University of Pennsylvania Library. In 1905 he completed a long novel, *Builders in Sand*, which was read by a friend of his brother's, a man who worked in the publishing house of G. P. Putnam. Perhaps planning to exploit Frank as a prodigy, he recommended the book for publication, but Julius Frank very wisely withdrew it as something Waldo might later regret.

Before the end of his last year at De Witt Clinton, Waldo Frank had passed the entrance examination for Harvard, and he engaged a room, planning to enter in the fall of 1906, but his father decided he was too young (the rebellion in English class may have influenced his decision), and, after the family had spent the summer in Europe, he entered Waldo at Les Chaumettes Pension in Lausanne for the academic year 1906-7.

This Swiss school had students from a multitude of nations. Waldo Frank studied French intensively, for the first time getting an insight into French culture. He continued lessons on the 'cello, which he had begun studying some years before. The

main interest that evolved for him, however, was living the life
of a German student, travelling from University to University,
in a quest for the best teachers of philosophy. Coming from a
home that was culturally as much European as American, this
would have meant clinching the European in him. His father,
who was willing for Waldo to make his own choice in fundamental values, was tolerant; but the idea produced a violent
reaction from his level-headed brother. The scene is described in
the introductory essay to Frank's *In the American Jungle:*

> . . . my father would not have stood against my will. He was an
> imperious, passionate man, whose prime passion was respect for
> the personality of others. A tyrant in matters of deportment, he
> hated all interference in adventures of the spirit. He had watched
> me, perhaps amused, perhaps with a hidden pang, go about at the
> age of twelve with my undigested load of Ibsen and Zola and
> Tolstoi. He had observed me, bored with school, become a truant,
> frequent the vaudeville shows or barricade myself from furious
> teachers in the office of our high school paper. Now, when the for-
> mal papers came from Heidelberg, telling the young American that
> he knew enough to be admitted, my father would not have said no,
> whatever his conviction. But my older brother was less philo-
> sophical. . . .
> "You are not going to Heidelberg," said my brother. "You are
> going to be an American, by gum! And what's more, you are not
> going to Harvard. You're queer enough as it is. You're going to be
> not only an American, but as *human* an American as I can make
> you. I'm going to send you to a place that will smooth out your
> angles and your crochets. Yale for you." . . . And to Yale I went.

Many sensitive and intellectual young people enter college
with too high expectations, become quickly disillusioned by the
less talented people present in the faculty and dominant among
the students, and expend their college life in pointless rebellion.
If Scott Fitzgerald had made the football team at Princeton the
literary history of the American twenties might have been differ-

ent. Waldo Frank, however, knew what he was getting into and accepted it. He made as many friends as any discriminating person does in college, and his social life was as much among the faculty as among the students. He completed work for the bachelor's degree in three years yet stayed to graduate with his class, taking the bachelor's and master's degree simultaneously in 1911. In his last year he was drama critic for the New Haven *Courier*, occasionally taking W. L. Phelps or W. E. Hocking, or some other faculty member or student to see the play with him.

From the weekly papers for Phelps's American Literature course, one would judge Frank to have been a superior but not startling scholar. However in 1908 he started a notebook listing the books he read, carefully indicating which he was reading for the second time. Although the list itself is formidable, it is even more impressive to realize that before he entered college he had read most of Shakespeare, Fielding, Sterne, Samuel Johnson, Goethe, Lessing, Ibsen, and all that was then published by Shaw. There are 1043 books and plays listed, and in a note at the end of the list Frank regrets not having started his notebook sooner since, he says, "it omits these [sic] years preceding in which I really did my most ravenous and fundamental reading. For, from fifteen to nineteen, I read more books in a year than is equalled in any year ensuing."

Although the list includes modern fiction that was little known at the time, among it the work of Romain Rolland, drama dominates. Probably every play that was in the Yale library at the time is down in Frank's list. Toward the end, the reading of Strindberg seems to have inspired Frank to investigate mystical philosophy and to have led him eventually to the Orientals, but the French drama seems to have attracted most of his attention, and eventually this attention resulted in Frank's second unpublished book, *The Spirit of Modern French Letters*.

The book was submitted to the Yale University Press, but it

was not until March, 1912, that the director, George Parmly
Day, requested certain revisions before recommending it for
publication. By that time Frank was engaged in other activities,
and when he did return to the book, his opinions had changed
so much that, although his notebooks contain outlines and notes
for years to come on a book to serve in its place, the project was
finally abandoned. One might say that the book grew out of
Frank's desire to be in the midst of the activity of the drama, to
be writing, and to be in France. In time that desire was satisfied
by more direct means.

The summer after his graduation from Yale, Waldo Frank
travelled through the West, but in the fall he returned to New
York. Armed with recommendations from the editor of the
Courier, he went about the newspaper offices, planning to
become drama critic and eventually to write plays. The *Post*
took him on as a reporter, and later he shifted to the *Times*, but
he was dissatisfied with both jobs. Neither seemed to be leading
him toward what he wanted; his only contact with literature
and drama came from interviewing people engaged in those
activities. Although at Yale he had begun writing stories that
he felt might be suitable for publication, and it is clear that he
had definitely chosen authorship as his career, he had difficulty
in settling down for the essential apprenticeship in writing. He
left his parents' home and took a furnished room, but living there
and working as a journalist he still felt unable to do what he
preferred. Therefore, like the expatriates of the twenties, he
chose Paris as a cheap and stimulating place to work.

Writers need the company of other writers, but not too much
of it. Moreover, they need to need each other, to create an
atmosphere comparable to the intellectual community of the
university, where they may stimulate each other and their collective thinking can find expression in the individual work of
each. There were American artists in Paris in 1912-13, but they

were intellectual as well as physical expatriates; they were the generation of Eliot and Pound and Gertrude Stein, who were to become permanent residents in Europe, returning to America only as visitors, separating themselves wholly from the milieu of America. Waldo Frank was not at home with them. He found French literary life more congenial, especially since he was introduced into it by a Frenchwoman who, as he says, "took me in and made me part of it."

He wrote profusely, chiefly plays. His notebook for this time, however, contains many themes for fiction, usually set in New York. For all of his close contact with Europe, never since his decision to go to Yale had he considered being other than American. America was his material, and although he had saturated himself in America during the previous summer and lived through the winter alone in New York, he had in the meantime completed the transition from college student about to become a writer, to journalist, to independent adult engaged in being a writer. France gave him an artistic milieu in which to work, but he and his writings were not part of it. As he puts it: "I was happy here, but I was not needed. I was being nourished by what other men, through centuries and ages, had created. I was a parasite. At least, so it seemed to me."

Back to New York he came, his bag full of plays and stories. He took a room on Washington Place, and entered into the life of Greenwich Village, then very much like Paris, but American (at least, after a fashion), and continued to write, beseiging the magazines with his stories, the producers with his plays. He had learned that becoming a writer requires an investment of much time and some money, and he had the means to submit his productions properly, hiring an agent, having his plays typed and copyrighted, and circulating stories with a careless disregard for the cost of postage. This was, however, 1913, not 1923. There were few theater groups, no magazines receptive to new writing except the often-shifting *Smart Set*. Moreover,

Frank had just returned from Europe, having refreshed his normal disregard for the taboos and prudery of pre-war America. Of nine stories written in 1913, none were published; of four plays, one, *The Key*, was accepted two years later by Alla Nazimova for vaudeville, and, after she abandoned it, by Helen Freeman's *Nine O'Clock Theater* in 1916—but never produced.

The Key is typical of most of the writing Frank was doing at this time; it attempts to reach a popular audience by superficial simplicity, but fundamentally it is based on such different values that it is like a tragedy given in a burlesque theater. The play tells of an American woman, married to a Venetian aristocrat, who admits her former suitor, an American, to her bedroom during a party. The American locks the door and throws the key into the canal. Since the only exit other than the locked door is the window overlooking the canal, the couple will be discovered by her husband who, according to the code of Venice, will kill them both. The American hoped that, their hours being numbered, his beloved would succumb to him. She sees things another way: can he swim? No? Too bad; he must jump into the canal anyway, to save her, and drown. At the last moment chivalry wins out, and he jumps. The play was obviously too daring then; too romantic for an age that would not think it too daring.

The Key for all its faults, is a surprisingly finished work to be written in the first year of a writer's apprenticeship. Nineteen fourteen was an even better year. Before it was half gone, Frank had nearly finished a long novel, *The Sisters*, part of which was published in *Smart Set* in December, 1915. A long story, *The Fruit of Misadventure*, the first work of 1914, was published in the same magazine in July, 1915, and a short article on the musician Leo Ornstein was published in *The Onlooker* in April, 1915.

A kind of transition took place in 1914. Up to the spring of that year Waldo Frank had been working very hard to break

his way into the magazines and the theater, determined to be
a success in the conventional sense. Although the confusion of
popular, financial success with artistic success was obviously a
result of his middle-class upbringing, he might have done it. The
sale of two stories to *Smart Set*, the magazine reputed to be the
most sophisticated of the time, indicates that he had learned his
craft. Mencken recognized him as a "comer," and when he
started the *American Mercury*, Frank was among the first writers
he asked to contribute. In 1925 his articles written under the
pseudonym "Searchlight" were a regular feature of the *New
Yorker*. He was gaining access, in other words, to the "smart"
market that was just coming into being, and had he chosen to
develop the vein of the first half of 1914, he probably could have
become one of the popular writers of light fiction. He chose,
however, to change direction, and the third part of *The Sisters*, a
novella called *Mary*, written in March of 1914, was the turning
point.

Whether this was a conscious choice or not is hard to say.
A writer, even of potboilers, has to express a *weltanschauung* in
his work; if he is cynical, he can fabricate a false philosophy of
platitudes to correspond with what he thinks his readers want.
Waldo Frank is not clever in that way, as his actions and writings from his revolt in the schoolroom to his recent pleas and
programs in the *Nation* clearly show. His brother's testimony
indicates that he was independently seeking a meaning in life,
through religion, as far back as 1901. Rather than taking the
method of his father, he chose Thoreau and Tolstoy as his aids
in that seeking. At Yale, and after, he continued his quest into
mystic philosophy and the religions of the East. In 1913, with
the reading of Bernard Hart's *The Psychology of Insanity*, a
new field opened to him. Soon he had read all of Havelock
Ellis, Freud, and Jung. Moreover, his interest in psychology
was stimulated by his finding a like-minded companion, Margaret Naumburg, who founded the Walden School, the first

to use the learning of the psychoanalysts, in 1914. With his own thinking strongly influenced by Viennese psychology, it is no wonder that he began using this material in his writing, and it was too soon for that to be acceptable to the reading public.

Frank today considers *The Way of Mary* his first serious fiction. It is the story of a girl who wished to be a sister to men, not in the sense of the cliché, but in the clinical sense. *The Sisters*, which included *The Way of Mary* with three other novellas, went the rounds of the publishing houses, but was rejected by all. Sinclair Lewis, who was then a reader for Doran, saw the potentialities in Frank's use of the new psychology, and encouraged him to try another novel. The moment for conscious decision had arrived. In the beginning of 1915 Frank found himself after three years of work a would-be popular writer with no stories published, no plays in production. He could not know that acceptances would start coming that year. Moreover, there was stirring around him the beginnings of an artistic renaissance. People were doing new things in new ways, hoping to be heard, to be read, but not compromising for it. Thus on the eve of popular success, Frank repudiated it to move from the story for the sake of the story, to the story as a psychological demonstration.

3

Toward the Lyric—I

AS EARLY AS 1915, WHEN HE COMPLETED *The Unwelcome Man*, four streams can be traced running concurrently through the fiction of Waldo Frank: the psychological, the social, the mystic, and the esthetic. From novel to novel, one or another of these may seem to the reader more obviously present than the others, but as Frank's work became organically unified, the four were integrated into the concept of the Person. Integration took place three separate times in Frank's career as a novelist, each time marking a step further toward an all-encompassing view of the cosmos in relation to its parts. In the lyric novels Frank shows the person in relation to the cosmos. The symphonic novels, as he calls them, relate both the person and society to the cosmos through a contrapuntal handling of themes comparable to that in the musical symphony; but the person and society remain separate. In preparation for the third step, both Frank's cultural studies and his transitional novels move toward making an organic whole of person, society, and cosmos. His most recent novel, *Not Heaven*, returns to the form of *City Block*, and unhampered by time and space benchmarks, achieves the unity. God is revealed within society simultaneous with God within the person.

Each new form was arrived at through constant experimentation in both fiction and non-fiction, and no sooner was each new form achieved than it was abandoned, while Frank went on to create another. This sequence follows the personal development of Waldo Frank, but was carried on with complete disregard for the development of literary taste in the United States. Often, even in his less successful books, Frank anticipated a future development in American fiction. One such occasion was *The Unwelcome Man*, with its almost clinical use of Freudian psychology. In Frank's career, however, it merely provided the training ground where he worked out the fundamentals of his method of characterization, and it carried him further toward use of fictional materials as a means of expression. Without being a part of the first step, the lyric novels, it prepared the way for that step. As a medium for the symbolic expression of an organic view of life, it is a failure; not until after the stock-taking of *Our America* was Waldo Frank able to formulate an organic view of life.

Although he is obviously the title character of *The Unwelcome Man*, and his experiences are drawn on for the details of the book, the story of Quincy Burt is not the story of Waldo Frank. He seems rather to have made Quincy experience only the disillusioning part of his life, and he gave Quincy more unpleasantness and despair to suffer than he had suffered. The story seems basically to be made up: Frank imagined himself an unwelcome eighth child in a shabby genteel Long Island family that later came into wealth and moved to Manhattan—the Upper West Side, of course. He gave one brother, Jonas, the characteristics that irritated him in his own brother, and gave the cripple Marsden his brother's gentler characteristics. He reported actual events in his life, such as the fight with his brother in their top-floor bedroom, even to the detail of the thrown hairbrush. He reports his disillusionment when his brother and sister find interests in their lives which exclude him. He even reports running away from home and his return for his mother's sake. He did not, however, draw on the ways of his

father and mother for the parents of Quincy Burt; the fictional
characters are much simpler people, well-meaning but insen-
sitively selfish, and neither understanding nor capable. Part
One, the childhood of the Unwelcome Man, is contrived and
comes to life only in its reportage of events in the childhood of
Waldo Frank. Moreover, except as clinical psychology, it is un-
important. That the parents of Quincy Burt bought twin beds
after his birth, so unwelcome was he, and completely forgot
him shortly afterward when he was sent to a nurse's during
the illness of two other children, is material for the psychological casebook, but does not become art.

Part Two, Quincy's college years, is a self-sufficient novella
which does not seem to be based on Frank's experiences at all,
although the setting could easily be Yale and the characters Yale
students and teachers. As we have seen, Frank did not need to
be disillusioned about the false popular values of college fraternity and athletic life, yet Frank makes Quincy painfully
undergo this sad experience. For the positive side of Quincy's
college life Frank did use some of actuality, making composites
of some of his friends into the two other important male
characters. For example, Frank got to know William Lyon
Phelps through Phelps's cordial response to an article he wrote
for the *Yale Courant*. This incident is recounted, with some
changes to make it fit the composite of Phelps, W. E. Hocking,
and possibly some others, from which he constructed the character of Professor Deering. A cosmopolitan Englishman Frank
met on a liner, blended with some of his literary friends of
Greenwich Village, produced Simon Garstead, Quincy's college
friend.

The technique involved is one fundamental to Frank's creative method. Taking real people—himself, his teachers, his
friends—he imagined different backgrounds for them and placed
them in situations that would tend to develop them in a
particular way. Since the argument of the college section is that

the unwelcome child will find the world rejecting him and yet will struggle to make himself welcome, failing because the lack of a welcome is a part of himself rather than being external, the chief character-warp is that of Frank's image in the book, Quincy. Quincy's greatest development is his discovery of a New York City that is more than the middle-class Upper West Side. Urged by Garstead, Quincy visits New York, avoiding the part he knows, walking from the Battery through lower Manhattan. It was a profound experience, condensed from Frank's own wanderings ever since 1906, when Hunter's *Poverty* sent him on similar journeys. When Quincy discussed it, back at college, Garstead asked him why he failed to divorce the sense of beauty from even the most squalid thing he saw. Quincy gropes for his answer and is prompted:

> "You don't seem to know what the sense of beauty means."
>
> "Let me see if I can figure it out." Quincy knit his brow, and his blue eyes softened. It was as if he had spiritually relaxed, instinctively aware that in this way one can receive.
>
> "Perhaps," he groped on, "perhaps, when I feel beauty, I am really feeling a sense of welcome. A welcome of the spirit."
>
> "Good!" cried Garstead. "And when do we welcome? Now, look out for your answer! No sentimentalism. Hypothetically, we welcome when we are charitable, altruistic, Christian. But actually—"
>
> "When we want, I guess."
>
> "We feel a sense of welcome, when we feel a sense of oneness. . . ."

Quincy's development into the unity with the world that would make him feel welcome was broken by the test and shock that might have completed the development—a completely imagined portion, with a character so completely amalgamized from Frank's then quite narrow acquaintance with women that she cannot be identified with anyone who actually lived, yet who contains the essence of womanhood and a rebelliousness that gives her many of the characteristics Frank was later to attribute to the Person. In subsequent novels, Frank was to base female characters on actual women, but the identification is possible only through careful examination of his notes; it is as if he borrowed only a potentiality in the character and from it developed a new creation. Julia Deering, a young wife imagined for the composite Professor Deering, became attracted to Quincy and competed with her husband for him. The affair between her and Quincy ended when she did not succeed in seducing him. That, and his confession to Professor Deering, broke the back of his development and his college career.

Part Three is mere dénouement, in which the identity of Quincy as a person is annihilated as he becomes a part of the business life of New York. Dramatically, toward the end he purchased a revolver intending to commit suicide, but rather than use it he chose to exist without life.

A tendril of his consciousness, faint yet infinitely fine, went out to the world of people. All of a sudden, he knew that they were dead. He knew that they long had been dead. They ate and laughed and danced—the dead. They builded cities on the murmurous landscapes and haunted the free waters of the sea—the dead. They had sonorous names for the rhythm of their rotting—the dead. He —had been alive. He had not been one of them. He had suffered. He had been unwelcome. But now? What was the easeful languor through him, the warmth that swathed him, the fellowship that buoyed him? He no longer suffered. He was one of them. He was dead also! He had found the way!

All that remained to seal his brotherhood was to forget even that he had found it, to forget even that he was dead, to walk the way blankly, blindly. All of his dead life remained for doing that. The battle had been waged! . . .

Beginning as a psychological study, with its symbols those of psychoanalysis, the novel shifts its emphasis through an esthetic technique—the creation of characters—to express Frank's then groping ideas on the concept of the Person. The author's failure to resolve his thinking results in Quincy's failure to achieve himself as a person. The lack is religious; Frank had yet to make clear to himself the place of the mystic. When Quincy came in contact with the world, represented by the business office in which he worked, by his courtship of Clarice Lodge, a girl as bound in social activities as a businessman is in his office, and by the city he grew up in but never became a part of, he was able to sense his need for further growth but was unable to do more than shrink back into the current of the city, losing Clarice, becoming alienated from his family, losing himself, becoming one in an endless row of men distinguishable only by their neckties or other details of façade, like the rows of nearly-identical brownstones.

The mystic lack in Quincy is represented most directly by erotic symbols. In his notebook Frank commented, "The Religion of To-morrow must be phallic, even as was the Religion of Yesterday." Quincy has no satisfactory relation with Julia Deering, although he spends a night with her; he will not replace the mother-symbol he sees in her with that of the lover. We see clearly the psychological profile of Quincy; we study his history and discover exactly what made him that way; we watch him as he makes the only resolution possible short of suicide, merging himself as a digit into society. He fails to be more than a symbol of a choice Waldo Frank might have taken but did not. Frank did not, for he was not Quincy Burt; Quincy lacked the positive development, particularly the artistic and sensitive family that Waldo Frank had. He did not, for he began to have success in his career after he had given up trying to adapt himself to the popular market. And he married Margaret Naumburg in December, 1916.

In addition to the flaw in Quincy, there is a dramatic inevitability, had Quincy become a person, that Waldo Frank could not then have handled successfully. In order to grow, Quincy had to make Julia his mistress. Adultery is a difficult thing to handle in realistic fiction; twice as difficult if the betrayed husband is an admirable character. To satisfy his own philosophy, which contained an erotic mysticism, and to express his concept of the Person who can escape losing himself in the stream of things, Waldo Frank had to find a new technique, one that would enable him to integrate his psychology and his mystic sense in the proper esthetic form. Like Quincy, he had to come out of the brownstones, and himself live the life he wished to express.

Waldo Frank's first successful experiment in the form of the novel evolved over a period of nine years. During that time he went through a transition brought on not only by the irresolution shown in *The Unwelcome Man*, but also by the founding of the *Seven Arts* magazine, American participation in the Great War, surveillance of the editors by federal agents because of the magazine's anti-war attitude, suspension of publication, and a severe illness followed by a time of personal depression. Before he found his form he produced another novel, *The Dark Mother*, and his greatest popular success, the cultural study, *Our America*.

Only a few months after completing the first draft of *The Unwelcome Man*, Frank was writing short stories that would eventually become part of *City Block*, the first of the lyric novels. The earliest of these, "Candles of Romance," was written in December, 1915, but was not published until February, 1917, in *Smart Set*. In January, 1916, "His Head Up" was finished, and it was published in W. R. Benét's *Chimaera* in May. After considerable revision, the story was re-named "Rudd," and published in the *Seven Arts* in August, 1917. In *City Block* it was called "The Table." "The Altar of the World" was written in March, 1916, but not published anywhere but in *City Block*. The first sketch for "John the Baptist" was finished in June, 1916, as a five-hundred-word sketch called "Tether-Ball." No more *City Block* stories were written until 1920, although notes for all of them were made at the same time as the notes for those finished in 1915-16, and the plan of the book was laid out for the first time.

Waldo Frank's Notebook VI, dated from July, 1914, to September, 1918, contains themes for forty-seven short stories. On the last few leaves are outlines for two volumes of short stories, one labelled "A Minute's Walk in Manhattan. A City Block." The plan called for fourteen stories, with page references to the notes for those not already written. Since "Bread Crumbs," written April, 1916, is the latest one without a page reference, and the earliest story with such a reference was started by Frank in June (neither of these stories appeared in the final version), the plan of a novel made of short stories written around a common theme can be dated in the middle of 1916. The notebook contains many references to Balzac, short comments and criticisms, suggesting that the story cycle idea was derived from the *Comédie Humaine*. Before *City Block* was finished, in 1922, the sequence of the stories in the cycle had changed, and the stories themselves were extensively revised, but the unifying theme and title, suggested by the block of flats in which Frank lived in the winter of 1915, were decided on at this early stage. 520 East Seventy-Seventh Street was a new low-rent housing project, and its block, east of Avenue A (now York Avenue) contained the city in microcosm, and is not much different today. Small shops line the avenue; on the block above is a public school; and to the east is a small park overlooking the river. The eight-story apartment houses that make up the project still stand out from the shabby tenements of the neighborhood, although today they do not attract people from as many parts of the city as they then did.

Appointment as associate editor of the *Seven Arts*, in the fall of 1916, interrupted Frank's creative activity, for editorial duties and article-writing for the magazine took up his time until it

suspended publication a year later. In the first issue appeared
Frank's article, "Emerging Greatness," on Sherwood Anderson,
whose *Windy McPherson's Son* had just been published. Anderson responded with a cordial letter, offering some short stories
he had written. "I made last year a series of sketches of people
of my home town, Clyde, Ohio," he wrote to Frank on November 14, 1916. "In the book I called the town Winesburg,
Ohio. . . . There are or will be seventeen of these sketches. Fifteen are I believe completed. . . . when these studies are published in book form they will suggest the real environment
out of which present day American youth is coming."

Frank and Anderson had each arrived around the same time
at the idea of a story cycle. When Anderson suggested that the
Seven Arts print all the Winesburg sketches, Frank clearly
understood what sort of work they were, for he replied on November 17 that there was not space to print them all in one
issue, and printing them as a series seemed to him unsatisfactory.
Realizing that they might be entities, however, if the overall plan
was not considered, he suggested that Anderson send them,
promising to do what he could. Eventually several of the Winesburg sketches were published in the *Seven Arts*.

The entry of the United States into the war was the end of
the *Seven Arts*, for the magazine had taken a pacifist position,
and pressure was brought that lost the editors their financial
support. Before the last issue, however, Frank was incapacitated
by illness that was incorrectly diagnosed, resulting in an operation that almost killed him and leading to a long period of
convalescence from which he emerged fully only in September,
1918. Early in 1918 he had started work on another novel, *The
Dark Mother*, that was to bring him a little closer to his new
form, but not to its achievement.

4

Toward the Lyric—II

IN *The Dark Mother*, INTEGRATION OF THE PSYCHOLOGICAL WITH the mystic is begun, social problems receive some treatment, and an esthetic begins to take shape. The germ of Frank's intention is shown in a notebook entry made near the beginning of 1916. The idea is for a story showing the parallel lives of a scoundrel and a saint, who follow separate courses and come together at the end in degradation, the scoundrel failing because his cleverness leads him to dare too much, the saint because of his "basic purity and inability to compromise or truckle."

Waldo Frank, like most of us, has always been interested in the clever fellow whose daring eventually overreaches his ability. This sort of character, usually a lawyer, turns up in six of his twelve novels, usually charming as a youth, and more corrupt the older he becomes. The saint and his problem of surviving in the world without sacrificing his sainthood is the central problem of ten of the twelve novels, and satisfactory answers appear only in the fully integrated ones.

In *The Dark Mother* the attempt at integration fails, for neither the scoundrel, Tom Rennard, nor the saint, David Markand, comes to any definite resolution of his problem. Indeed, their problems are hardly posed, for the psychological development of the characters, and their potential homosexual relationship, took Frank's attention away from his original objective and caused him to add a major female character, Tom's sister Cor-

42

nelia, as a mother image for David and a symbol of incest for Tom. A situation that one might call the unnatural triangle is set up, with David being attracted to Tom through potential homosexuality, and attracted to Cornelia as a substitute mother. Tom and Cornelia return David's interest, and are incestuously attracted to each other. The buildup of this triangle, its tenuous existence until one of the attractions overpowered the others or an outside attraction upset the balance of forces, resulting in the disintegration of those left, would probably have been the psychological study Frank would have written if he had not progressed beyond *The Unwelcome Man*.

In transition, he not only added social problems, but complicated the psychological by a multitude of attractions between David and various women. The triangle is thus midway between being the central tension of the book and being merely a stage in the development of David. Efforts toward integration are made through experimentation in the form of the scene, but since the overall pattern of the novel is conventional, this attempt too goes only half way. David is carried far toward becoming a Person, aware of his place in the cosmos but retaining his identity; Tom is carried past the point where he can do so; and Cornelia, lost when the triangle is broken, commits suicide. These climaxes and resolutions are, however, based on sound psychology rather than dramatic necessity, so they come about by evolution rather than sudden change, and the point of revelation is always mystic. Thus, in a novel outwardly naturalistic, which should mark its climaxes with external conflict even when the conflict is only symbolic of an internal struggle, purely internal mystic resolutions seem unreal, their actions seem forced, and nothing seems to have happened. The reader is led to expect one thing, and when he does not find it, he is not satisfied. Before Frank would be able to communicate the world as *he* saw it, he had to create not only a new attitude toward characters and a new style, but a new overall structure as well.

In The Dark Mother Frank's purpose was not reflection of
the external world, but rather analysis of the interaction of the
person and his surroundings. That interaction is more than
physical, more than mental. It relies on deeper insights on the
part of the author, insights that are in the nature of revelation.
Its ultimate function in Frank's fiction is to show the development of a character into a Person, acting in awareness of the
community of all things, never confusing the part with the
whole. For Waldo Frank, the achievement of utter clarity on
how to apply this concept to the complicated matter of life,
indeed the ultimate meaning of the concept itself, comes as a
mystical experience. In The Dark Mother David Markand has
such a moment after a walk through the city fills him with a
sense of belonging with the women and children on their door-
steps:

> Blackness . . . ultimate texture of all colors . . . light. A world of
> infinite color, infinite flesh: himself within the world, himself
> carried within it through it. Himself of the breakless tissue of the
> world. Flesh of sweet smells, sweet odors, sweet fluids. Flesh alto-
> gether and altogether about him. He altogether touching all
> flesh—and All. David knew through his shut eyes, walking
> the world, how he was carried within a world of ceaseless
> substance: how he was substance within it: how his moving
> and knowing through Flesh was Spirit. . . . He walked—he
> worked—he ate. He had a woman's body, he earned the bread of a
> man, he held the love of a friend. Flesh, all. And his moving
> through Flesh, through the world of Flesh—Spirit and Dawn. . . .
> His eyes were shut. But his mouth was open! David saw with his
> mouth. And though he knew not he had seen, there was within
> him, there would be now forevermore within him, life of a vision.
>   The world was a Dark Mother. The Night of the miracle of
> worlds was fleshed and was a Mother. She moved in infinite direc-
> tions an infinite path. She was moveless. And he within her, moving
> with the world toward the movelessness of birth.
>   David was unborn. But his mouth sucked vision. Sucking the

Night sucked vision. He slept again. Slept long. . . . Slept years. . . .
But he lived.

This vision, however, does not seem to be a whole one. It is
imperfect as the novel is imperfect. It is too fleshed; like the
novel it is too full of the flesh of motherhood; it is a spiritual
glimpse clothed in the ludicrous symbols of a pregnant woman
and a sucking baby—ludicrous because, in a novel with the outward form of a realistic reflection of the physical world, the
reader is not prepared. Disturbing connotations are attached to
the word *suck*, and the whole effect is like an attempt at hyp-
nosis that does not succeed.

In 1948, in an appreciation of Paul Rosenfeld, Waldo Frank
wrote: "A good novel is a poem, in which diverse tissues of
social and personal fact are essentialized into a unitary pattern."
In *The Dark Mother* the novel as a poem was taking shape, and
if it were wholly subjective, atmosphere could be built up that
would make passages like the one quoted not ludicrous at all.
The central characters are subjectively treated, their inner
thoughts and perceptions reflected in the mind of the author,
who is as omni-present in the book as a poet is in his poem.
The setting is described, not as it is, but as it affects the author,
sometimes as himself, sometimes as David, Tom, or Cornelia.
The words and their arrangement show careful attention to
sound. Waldo Frank is more ear-minded than eye-minded.
Physical objects, concrete details, are merely bench-marks, locat-
ing the subjective impression he presents. The music of his
language dominates the picture-making quality. Indeed, his descriptions, using sound and sense to create an impression of the
spirit of a place, rely on the reader's recognizing, not the picture,
but the atmosphere, and drawing from his experience the scene
that made him feel that way. This is one of the reasons that
translations of Frank's books have seemed almost like native
works in as diverse countries as Russia and Argentina.

But mixed with these subjectively-treated characters, each a facet of Waldo Frank, each speaking with the voice of Waldo Frank, each indistinguishable from Quincy Burt of *The Unwelcome Man*, as Paul Rosenfeld pointed out in *Men Seen*, are objectively-presented characters, who come to life as no characters do in *The Unwelcome Man*.

David's uncle, Anthony Deane, who brings him to New York after his mother's death and makes him prove himself in the tobacco business, is shy and solicitous when he acts as a person —visiting the Markands after David's father's death, greeting David on his arrival in New York, pampering his daughters and being dominated by his wife—but is vital and domineering when the world of affairs takes the place of human relationships. The morning after David's arrival in the city they breakfast together.

"We'll go down together, my boy—for the first day." He consulted his watch. "It's eight-twenty now. As a rule, I think Mr. McGill will want you at the office at eight. It takes forty minutes from here to the office. Fifteen minutes for breakfast." He reckoned and rang the bell. To the entering girl: "Anne, Mr. David's regular breakfast time will be ten past seven." . . .

"Does your watch keep good time?" he asked. Why should the question seem to bring him relief? "See to that, my boy. The City is run on *schedule*. On *schedule*. That's why it's a great City. That's what makes a great City out of a piece of country. Manhattan once had fields in it. And a few hills. Oh, yes—Central Park was a squatter's marsh. Wait till you see it with its new asphalt roads! Some day there'll be asphalt roads all over the country."

David, fresh from Connecticut, asks if asphalt roads are not hard on the horses. (The year is 1897.) This calls forth a rapture on the world of Anthony Deane:

. . . "you'll have to change your outlook on life, now that you are to become a part of the great City—a part of the great Machine. You'll be proud of it, soon enough. The New Yorker is a man of service. He serves Business. He serves Country. He don't think of himself. Look at me. . . . I've not taken three weeks off in twenty years' time. I stick to my guns. They can trust me in the City. They know I am faithful: I am always on the spot. The jolly easy ways of the country don't go far in the Metropolis. We're a beehive, we are. Work! Service! And the ambition of every man is to die in harness. Of course, I mean the men who *succeed*. That is the one way to earn real money in New York. To think of absolutely nothing else: to give time to absolutely nothing else. There's the American Ideal of Service for you." He paused and glowed upon his nephew who sat, stiffly erect, trying to believe, in order that he might like this talk. . . . "And, my boy, what's the result? Don't you know? . . . America is the result!" He flourished his white hands. "The great Democracy. The land of three and a half million square miles. We've made it. The American Ideal made it. I've been out West. I've seen our country. The Rockies that you could drop the Alps into—lose them. The Grand Canyon that's a mile from top to bottom. The geysers in Yellowstone Park. The greatest, most populous, the *biggest* country on Earth! And we've made it. We're making it, my boy. American Ideals."

Mr. Deane stopped again. He reached for his climax. He found it. "I presume," he said, "I presume no sane man will deny that William McKinley is the greatest statesman today in the world!"

And the same man, on the day of his family's arrival from the country, where they were when David came to New York, is no longer assured, no longer efficient, but bumbles about noisily puffing.

Mr. Deane had been quarreling with the coachman about the fare: his own carriage was not yet in service. He puffed into the room. David saw and at length realized how changed he was, in the true setting of his wife and daughters. He scarcely noticed David.

"Got everything?" he asked excitedly. "Nothing lost? My! it's hot! That robber robbed me. Lauretta—you have the keys? I must run along. Where's breakfast?" He mopped his brow, he paced; and David wondered whether the executive task of shipping his family to New York—or some obscure disturbance—was the thing too much for him.

Mr. Deane in his business office is still a third person, competent, purposeful, and sympathetic—truly in his element. This rounds out his character, makes the use of him for ironic comment on the "practical man" all the more effective, for he is so good a businessman and so uneasy a husband, father, and host that we see he really has thought of nothing but making money. He is, however, an incidental character, and as the book progresses, although he comes more clearly into focus, he falls farther and farther into the background.

Other incidental characters are equally well portrayed: the maid, who comforts David in his first lonely weeks in the city, eventually coming to his bed; Lois, one of the Deanes' two daughters, who forms a sister-image for David, yet stirs him physically; Miss Lord, known in Deane and Company as "a remarkable woman," who represents the "new woman," and is striving for social poise in the same way she went about learning the business; even the miscellaneous people who turn up at parties or appear and disappear almost as scenes of the city, in the background of David and Tom and Cornelia, ring true as realistic characters in a way that the central characters do not —mainly because they are scenes in the city, rather than parts of Waldo Frank striving toward wholeness.

David, the one of the three who succeeds, is cast like the other two into the city, whose many currents he must buck if he is to do more than disappear in it as did Quincy. Business, art, the circles of his friends, all buffet him in different directions. Woman after woman attracts him and attempts to sweep him along her way, and among the women is Cornelia. Tom tries to sweep him along, change him, "steal some of his innocence"; and in his effort to do so is diverted from his own love for Marcia Duffield. David's success is symbolized by his prospect, at the end of the book, of marriage with Helen Daindrie, who demands that he make his own current, that he make himself powerful for her, since she is already stronger than he and his rival is the superior Dr. Westerling. In one sense, the dark mother of the title is the city, an ominous mother, devourer of those, like Quincy and Tom and Cornelia, who are weak and fall in with a current; yet a giver of birth, a developer of strength in those who resist.

Another central character, then, is the city. And in characterizing the city, Waldo Frank uses the same method of presenting the surface with few concrete details but extracting the spirit, the essential, as he uses in presenting the central characters who are people. Because we have no conventions for the characterization of a city as we do for the characterization of people, we are more willing to accept an internal image than we are to accept the same sort of characterization of a person. Moreover, the city has no dialogue. In the character-portraits poetic abstraction of the inner tensions between people set side-by-side with a realistic reportage of the banality of ordinary conversation or commonplace events brings about let-downs that destroy the atmosphere. While Cornelia is losing to her brother the love of David, this occurs regularly, even though the actions are well-motivated psychologically. As she and David sit in her studio, memories of her childhood mix with the present, and she thinks of her father's smashing the sculpture he had puritannically forbidden her to make, of her brother's challenging her to balance a stick on end, one that he had secretly tied a string to, so he would pull it over when she had it almost in balance. The bust becomes David, the stick her father, and the stick falls to smash the bust.

> The mood held. She remained in that palpitant hinterland where all the nerves and senses of herself met all the beings of her past. David impinged sweetly upon this swerving world. She lay, scarce breathing, looking at him with eyes that denied the rest of her.

The world where he could thrust in his head without violence receded. It went. Again, her senses were enemies, strangers. That was a man to whom she had not given herself. Her senses stormed her recovering mind. "Why does he not take me in his arms?" they pleaded. She was on her feet, shutting herself away.

"How you frightened me, David! I guess I fell asleep."

A few lines further on, the contrast between the interior dialogue and the exterior commonplaceness is even greater:

She looked at him.

Big, burly boy, with his blue muffler over his throat and his hands hanging so limp beside him. He was so at ease, so friendly curious, so cool. While she was white inside with the need of telling. It was impossible. In the shadow, a pain viced Cornelia's homely face— lent accent to the wrinkles already upon her brow. It went, leaving its sharp bite.

"How have you been, David?

The climax to the scene is climax also in these jarring contrasts:

She left him to put on her hat. She saw herself in the mirror: plain Cornelia, Motherer! who had found her boy at the age when boys go forth. Her mouth affirmed the bitter resolution that must make it hard: her eyes fought against their tears—David was there —with a dry will that must dull and dim them. The ineffable glow of confidence and of the sense of being sweet faded still farther from her face, leaving it older and less sweet.

So she returned to David: they went out to dine.

Frank's intention in the scene of which we have seen three excerpts is a valid and important one. The contrast between Cornelia's inner passion and the restraint which she imposes on her behavior before David is a necessary part of the history of their relationship. But the effect is lost because the commonplace dialogue and action, made up entirely of stereotypes, utterly destroys the credibility of the more important inner action and dialogue. Where this abstraction of the essence of a situation is used other than with people, or with silent people, leaving out the banal, it is productive of very unusual effects. By means of it, New York is made an organism, vital, ominous, creative. David walks down Wall Street:

> Glass casements fronting heavy buildings, huge masonry pillared by slender stone—the grace and loom, the hypocrisy of power. Spawn of the buildings: men with naked singing nerves like wires in a storm, and women with dead eyes, women with soft breasts against a hard tiding world. Furious streets. A street wide and delirious with men shouting and waving their straw-hats like banners. Streets narrow and somber that curled like smoke across his feet. Streets eaten with secret moods. Streets cluttered and twisting with pent power. Streets pulsant like hose. Streets slumbrous like pythons. Streets writhing and locked.
>
> A wide gash of sky. The sun was a stranger. The blue was a burn.
>
> They went toward the River. Black houses were lost among the masts of ships. Black herded houses crawled towards the wharves. Men were nervous like rats feeding on grain.

This is not realistic, although a reader familiar with the financial district of New York City can recognize the route David followed; it is a poetic flight, in which we are not shown the physical objects, but the emotional effect those objects had on the writer. The people in the scene are presented with the same subjective method as that used with Cornelia in the scene previously quoted from; yet before the method produced ludicrous effects, and here it is successful. The inclusion of realistic conversation or reportage of commonplace actions clashes inevitably with such poetic flights. The effect is ironic, and irony tends to upset the meaning of statements.

Irony is used to very good effect in producing the social criticism of the book, and it is quite possible that the irony that destroys the effect of many of the lyric passages is intentional, the result of imperfect integration of social criticism into the

conception of the characters. Those corrupted by the city, stunt-
ing their human qualities for success, get no pity from Waldo
Frank, although he sympathetically presents the human quality,
however slight it may be, in all of them. The ironic peak, clearly
developed from the original theme for the novel as it was laid
down in Notebook VI, comes in a scene at a shabby Italian
restaurant, a sort of semi-club, where all the customers mingle
like guests at a party. David listens to a conversation between
Tom and a cynically brilliant man named Korn who quotes
Goethe to Tom's comment, "The more rules, the more brains
to overturn them." Tom toasts the logic in Korn's life, indicating that he and Korn have similar lives, but that Korn's is more
consistent. Tom is succeeding as a lawyer; Korn, we learn with
David at the end of the scene, is a pickpocket. David is shocked,
and Tom replies that there are no sharp distinctions between
criminals and honest men. "Look about you," he says. "I don't
apologize for Korn. He is what he is. He is the typical social
being. Nakedly. The rest of us think we are the pretty names
we are called by."

For all the effectiveness irony can have, however, it is used
too frequently in *The Dark Mother*. The point is made too
often that people's speech and actions do not measure up to
their inner potentialities. The flaw is deep—so deep that one
suspects Frank himself was indecisive and had doubt about the
progress his characters were making. At the end of the book,
the balance of forces is upset by Cornelia, who, feeling that she
is losing David, rather than surrender him to Tom, encourages
him toward an affair with Helen Daindrie. When it becomes
clear that she has lost David to Helen, even though Tom has
lost him also, Cornelia commits suicide. We see David in
Helen's arms, and the last line of the book, Helen's words that
admit him to her love, are: "I am so eager to have my family
really know you." That final note is so banal that we have difficulty believing that David is finding a better relationship. David

got no farther because Waldo Frank had progressed only to that point in his quest of wholeness. From the perspective of today, knowing that in *The Death and Birth of David Markand* David would progress beyond Helen, moving on to become a whole person to the same extent that Waldo Frank had in fifteen more years, we can consider *The Dark Mother* an incomplete work. Disregarding that later development, we can consider the novel as complete but imperfect, with the inherent flaw of a technique that does not fit its form.

The technique of scene-making, however, developed in *The Dark Mother*, is a real step toward the lyric novels that followed. A scene will begin in a place, at a time, and then will flash back to the circumstances that brought the characters to that place at that time, rather than keeping to a movie-shot sort of time-place unity. Chapter V is made of one such scene, with the function of showing the emotional context in which David turned to Cornelia and of symbolizing that Tom will turn him from her.

The frame of the scene is a visit Tom and Cornelia pay David after he has left the Deane home and taken a room by himself. We see the house, near Stuyvesant Square, and the street. We see Tom and Cornelia go up the steps, and in their ears we hear the sounds of the city. Inside the vestibule, Tom rings the doorbell, and we enter his thoughts as he notices the ugliness of the decoration and his mind flashes back to a scene between him and his new partner, showing the growth of corruption in Tom, an association in his mind of the ugliness in his life with the ugliness of the vestibule.

Tom and Cornelia enter the hall, thinking about the heat; and since David, in his room above them, is also thinking about the heat, we shift to him. His impressions of the room bring to mind the scene, in the mountains, when he told the Deanes he was going to leave their house. Images of the vacation-time suggest each other: Mr. Deane on vacation contrasted with Mr.

Deane at work. How he smokes cigars (chews them in the city; smokes them in the country), his greater ease with his family, a tennis game that included Lois. Relations with the Deane women enter David's mind, and they recall his desire to enlist for the Spanish-American War. Scenes made up of details unknown to David indicate that we have moved entirely out of the dramatic, even of the flashback: his uncle's subterfuges to keep him from enlisting, Tom's resistance to his going, and even a private interview between Tom and Mr. Deane show that the author is not just interested in revealing the mind of the character, but of spotlighting motives and relationships—the social and personal together—that created an event. The crux of David's memories about his wish to enlist is the reaction of Lois to his plans. A coolness grows between them, the result of too great physical attraction in a brother-sister relationship, until she accepts him "as part of the parade they had applauded together through the open window." This marks the end of his affection for her, and we are returned to David, waiting for Tom and Cornelia in his new room, with his real reason for leaving the Deanes' made more vivid for us than he could have known it—to get away from Lois.

David still has time to jump back in thought from Lois to his mother before Tom and Cornelia get up the stairs to his door, so that the leitmotif of the mother-image can announce Cornelia while the sister motif of Lois fades out. They enter, completing the juxtaposition of the four directions his affections have tended most strongly: the mother, the mother-substitute, the incestuous sister, and, in the person of Tom, the homosexual relationship.

The smallness of the room dismays Tom and Cornelia, and David, gay at their coming, gay at being free, gay in an effort to infect them with his gaiety, centers his attention on Cornelia. Tom, however, gloomy at realizing how crass he has become, chills David's enthusiasm, so that he drops Cornelia's hands.

Thus the past is presented and the future is symbolized, not in the dramatic form of current novels in which the author is not an active participant, but in the form of subjective analysis and demonstration of the emotional currents in the scene, carried out through the omniscient perceptions of the author and limited only by the author's own limitations.

In *The Dark Mother* Waldo Frank tried to do more things than he was capable of doing at the time. His attempt to demonstrate the growth of wholeness in the person was limited by a lack of certainty about what wholeness is in a person; and his inability to integrate social criticism with his insight into character prevented his work from becoming unified in effect. He had to take these problems up separately, and in time he would do so. With the completion of *City Block* his vision of the person would grow surer; and in *Our America* he would crystallize his social dream.

5

Our America

DURING THE WRITING OF The Dark Mother, FRANK HAD TAKEN time off to write a long essay about Jacques Copeau's Théâtre du Vieux Colombier, in the United States during the war, and under the title Art of the Vieux Colombier, it was published as a small paperbound book by the Nouvelle Revue Française. Frank's acquaintance with the work of the NRF group went back to his time in Paris before the war, and he had written about them in the Seven Arts. Although primarily concerned with their esthetic of play production, the book describes the formation of the NRF group and their rôle in the art of young France. Because their deeper motives had been expressed by Frank, and because they sensed the vitality in his vision of America, two members of this French "cultural mission to the United States," Copeau and Gaston Gallimard, requested him to write a book that would tell Frenchmen about their recent ally. It was, as Frank stated in his introduction for American readers, "to create channels between [Young America] and their own Young France."

Frank's experience with the literary radicals on the Seven Arts and the exercise of social criticism in writing The Dark Mother had clarified his ideas, and, as is indicated by his letters to Van Wyck Brooks, then in California, he wrote the book easily and rapidly. Begun early in 1919, the first draft was finished in April, and revision was done in May and June. In the meantime The

Dark Mother had been going the rounds of the publishers and was accepted by Boni and Liveright, who published it, after further revision, in October, 1920. When they were offered *Our America*, however, they put it immediately to production, issuing it in November, 1919. Eleven months later the French edition appeared.

Our America reached its readers at exactly the right time. The tenuous unity created by the war was beginning to break up, and various economic and social factors were already consolidating those concerned with ideas and ideals in opposition to "practical men." Radicals, intellectuals, and people interested in the arts found common cause through opposition to a negative puritanism, a tawdry prosperity, and man's increasing reliance on the machine and dominance by the machine-like in social organization. What John Reed, E. E. Cummings, Eugene Debs, and the organizers of the New School for Social Research had in common was opposition to the sterile, the materialistic, and the routine in the society emerging from the war. If one examines the speeches and writings of these figures, representative of the unorganized coalition against Babbitt, the principles of the English Romantics emerge. Thus *Our America*, which discusses social forces in esthetic terms and sums up each part of the country through its arts and its artists, was in key with the ideas that bound together what was essentially a quite divided group. Since its literary ancestor was Whitman's *Democratic Vistas* as much as it was Croly's *Promise of American Life* or Beard's *Economic Interpretation of the Constitution*, it was as much a vision of an America to be as it was analysis of contemporary society and its backgrounds.

Our America had a great success. While it was making a name for Waldo Frank throughout the country, he was travelling, through the Middle West in the last two months of 1919, and the South in January of 1920. He says now that he was running away from the invitations to lecture, to write articles, and in

other ways to exploit the thinking that produced *Our America*.
He obviously was troubled. Having achieved a popular success,
having clarified his view of a positive America, going through a
difficult stage in his marriage, feeling the emptiness of inactivity
in his life, he did not know what to do next. Many writers feel
this same disturbance after their first success, and with Frank
it was complicated by more than the "can I do it again?" doubt.
He wondered if he wanted to do it again.

While the book was on the press, Frank had been reading
intensively in the Medieval Jewish mystics and the Cabalists
down to Spinoza. He had previously rejected Judaism as a thing
bound up in ritual and backwardness, not through investigation,
but because his father had done so. Social conditions in America, after the large influx of Jews from Eastern Europe, had
forced upon American Jews of the earlier migrations an awareness of their Jewishness. Like many young men whose connection with Judaism had been exceedingly tenuous, Waldo Frank
resisted this awareness; since his father had rejected the older
religion for Ethical Culture, and he had progressed beyond his
father in every other respect, could he go back and accept what
his father did not? The way became clear for him in Richmond,
Virginia, in February, 1920, when he had three mystical experiences in the same number of weeks, and then a recurrence of
several such experiences.

Now, what is a mystical experience? Great intuitive thinkers
frequently enough have reported them, and therefore the rest of
us must acknowledge their validity. The pattern seems usually
the same. First comes the awareness of personal inadequacy—
the letdown after *Our America*—the "dark night of the soul";
and finally an illumination that cuts through the complications
of the mystic's problems with an experience leaving him full of
a sense of the unity of all things. The mystic feels personally
involved, with unity expressing itself through him. The result
of whatever happened to Waldo Frank in February, 1920, is,

at any rate, clear for us to see. For seven months before, he had
not written anything. Two months after the experience, he
had completed the whole first draft of *City Block*; seven months
after that he had finished *Rahab*; on page 69 of Notebook VII,
where experiences are recorded on pages 43-54, 63-66, is a complete outline of *Holiday*, including notes for the opening that
are very like the final form. Moreover, these novels show an
organic unity in form and content that was the greatest lack of
The Dark Mother, a unity that was made possible only by the
development of a similar harmony in the character of Waldo
Frank.

His spiritual problem had been on his mind for some time,
and most of the facts had been at his command. He showed
comprehension of the values of Judaism in his expository writings, although, significantly enough, in his fiction, where truth
about the author is never completely hidden, none of his major
characters were Jews. The mystical experiences seem to have
climaxed the sense of unity he had been groping for since his
experience with the cat when he was a child. It undoubtedly
was strengthened by his reading of Whitman. Exactly when he
identified it with the tradition of the Jews is difficult to say; but
the identification had been made rationally when he wrote
about the *unanimistes* of France in an essay on Jules Romains
in the *Seven Arts*.

Orthodox Jews express their feeling of the one-ness of all
things through a complicated ritual made out of the primitive su-
perstitions of their nomadic ancestors, their health rules, their
moral standards, and their social practices. Frank was probably
not aware, before he read Spinoza, that Jews had harmonized
the ideas behind the ritual with further developments in science
and philosophy. It is not that he took his ideas from Spinoza,
but he took Spinoza as model in centering his knowledge of
society, modern psychology, and phenomena of the material
universe on the unity he felt to exist; and once his concept of

the person could jibe with science, he could unify his esthetic form around it. The obstacle to his integrating the facts of psychology and sociology with the vision that had grown within him from childhood was his middle class liberal background—again, those brownstone rows of the Upper West Side. Religious liberalism, political liberalism, the materialistic view of the universe in which man is bounded by his rational powers: these he abandoned, to formulate a structure for his religious, political, social, esthetic, and ethical standpoints as one—the concept of the Person; and to express that concept in an esthetic created for the purpose—the lyric novel.

6

City Block

THE BOOKS THAT WALDO FRANK CALLED "THE LYRIC NOVELS" ARE *City Block*, *Rahab*, *Holiday*, and *Chalk Face*. The form came into being first, then was rationalized, described, and named. The word *lyric*, applied to a novel, derives, as does the word *lyric* applied to a poem, from music. Let us say that the lyric poem and the lyric novel have a common ancestor. A novel is not a poem; the lyric novel, however, has the same purpose as a poem—to express a subjective idea or vision directly from the consciousness of the writer through suggestion, rather than by direct statement. The lyric novel, like the poem, is an emotional rather than a rational experience, and unlike realistic fiction, its esthetic does not rely on reflection of life, but makes a more direct contribution to life.

The concept of the Person, the man aware of his unity with all things, living in terms of the Whole expressed through its parts, is the kind of idea that has been expressed most effectively in poetry. A character in literature who is a Person is very rare, as Aldous Huxley, who conceives of something comparable to the Person in his "non-attachment," has pointed out in *Ends and Means*:

> But most of our literary examples, as we have seen, are mere idealizations of the average sensual man. Of the more heroic characters the majority are just grandiosely paranoic; the others are good, but good incompletely and without intelligence; are virtuous within a

bad system which they fail to see the need of changing; combine a measure of non-attachment in personal matters with loyalty to some creed, such as fascism or communism or nationalism, that entails, if acted upon, the commission of every kind of crime.

Indeed, in the novel which reflects life, the Person would not make an interesting character, for he lacks the flaw necessary to make an interesting, familiar, or significant struggle. In *The Unwelcome Man* Frank had to show the failure of his protagonist—show his individuality being erased—to express his idea. In *The Dark Mother* he was more successful in showing the failure of Tom and Cornelia than in showing the success of David; and the only symbol he could find for David's success was a healthy marriage. In *City Block*, however, by transforming the subjective method of description developed in the preceding novel into his method of narration, and by bringing in himself, both as "the man that wrote" the stories and as one of the characters, Frank wiped out the dramatic distance, moved the novel from its usual position of midway between poem and play, and shifted the center of interest from the character to the idea. Instead of seeing the characters as figures off on a stage, separated from us by the proscenium, we have moved to their very core and are prying deeply into their spirits, seeking that which they have in common. That shift not only makes the novel more like a poem in its effect, but justifies the name "novel" being applied to a collection of short stories. A novel has traditionally been a prose tale of some length unified about a character, group of characters, plot, place, time, or effect. Novels have gone unchallenged lacking any of these but the unifying effect of a single character or group of characters. Frank chose, in *City Block*, to unify primarily around the effect, but he kept time and place unity as well. Moreover, he tied the work together still more firmly by making characters central in one story appear incidentally in others, and by having the first story about a husband's quest for a Christmas present for his wife be complemented in the next to last story with the same man's wife seeking a gift for her husband. This poetic return appeals to the reader's sense of pleasure through familiarity in the same way as does the refrain of a poem. In a note preceding the first page the reader is warned that the stories are meant to be read in the order in which they appear, if the work is to sustain its unity. The emotional effect of each story is like the effect of each image in a poem like "The Waste Land," with the point of the whole work being made by leading the reader through a gamut of emotional experiences. If the images are rearranged in the poem, it no longer means what it once did.

City Block as lyric novel went through a long evolution. Both the plan and the story notes of 1916 indicate that what Frank had in mind at first was a small-scale Comédie Humaine. All the stories, as first sketched out in the notebook, are tragic, showing futility and irony in life. The plan was sociological—to reflect a geographical unity in the city. The published book, however, is nothing of the sort. The block has ceased to be a civic unit and has become a cosmic unit. The interplay of characters, both within the stories and between stories, has ceased to be ironic, but instead shows the spiritual interdependence of people. The only futility is in those characters who try to face life alone and barren. Most of the stories, and the work as a whole, show a victory over tragedy.

The first versions of the stories written in 1916 are ordinary philosophical fiction. They can be summarized in external action; indeed, rather than rely on symbolism, Frank in 1916 chose to insert an expository passage whenever the material became too subtle for dramatic handling. This is especially noticeable in the Smart Set version of "Candles." The story tells of a man who has drawn into himself and created a dream-ideal in place of his wife. When, through his neglect, his real wife dies, he finds that he can no longer envision the ideal—that the ideal was his wife's youth, and when she is gone, he can no longer recapture the image of what she was like when she was young. When the man, Godfrey Carber, formulates the image of his ideal, the story says that in so many words. Some symbolism is present, but it is accompanied by explanation. The story follows a straight chronology from Godfrey Carber's arrival in New York to take a teaching job, through his marriage, his wife's becoming a household convenience to him, the development of the dream, to her death. The significant part of the story is entirely in the final scene in which the dream dies with the wife, Dora; all the preliminaries are mere exposition.

In *City Block*, the whole of "Candles" is told from inside Godfrey Carber in two psychological stages that are fused together in the ending. At first, the story shows his lack of response to the magnitude of the city, his response to his pupils and Dora, who, like the pupils, has youth.

> No good things have names save myself and my wife Dora and my girls. Other names mean lies. School that does not teach a thing and that would be terrible void without my nameless caress: or New York that has no right to sound the least like Dora . . . these are examples.
>
> Now there's another name that doesn't mean a thing. Dora says to me: "Dear, I am going to have a child. We are going to have a child." She puts that name on us. And it doesn't mean a thing.

The child is stillborn, and Dora begins to lose her youth. Godfrey does not notice, still cherishes her, until a day in winter. He goes to visit the father of a pupil in the hospital, and coming from the presence of infirmity, needing to be refreshed by the sight of Dora in her youth, he rushes home in the snow, leaving the streetcar because it does not move fast enough.

> Here is the Block. Endless long. —How can my feet, pushing little fragments of the snow-full Block, push it behind me? Feet push . . . Feet push, behind, little bits of the Block. The flat looms

up. The stair looms up. The door is open ere he reaches it.
Dora! . . .

> —She is not young at all!
> Her eyes are heavy and dull!
> Her hair is no coil of Spring!
> Her breast sags! She sags!

Dazed, he seems ill, and the matronly Dora puts him to bed,
where the dream comes to him, comes between them:

> —She is full Springtime.
> Her hair coils like June.
> Her hands upon me
> Flower my flesh like June
> Her face is June
> Upon the earth of my longing . . .

As from the beginning of the story Godfrey Carber's love for
his wife was developed, so from this point is developed his love
for the dream-ideal. It grows; before long the real Dora is
resented as an intruder between him and his dream. He symbolizes the coming of the dream by shutting out the gas light
and lighting a candle. Dora realizes and accepts that she has
become mere housekeeper in his life, even to the extent that
she will not break into his dream by telling him she has learned
she needs an operation. Finally she collapses, and he learns of
her coming death. He carries candles to her bedside, finally
making the identification.

No longer is the ending the story, but the ending is merely
ending, the inevitable culmination of what came before. The
development of Godfrey Carber's spiritual state from his psychological state is the drama of the story. No longer do we see the
city block as a man in a skyscraper overlooking it might see it;
in the final form of the book we see the block as God might
see it.

Central in the book and a key to understanding the technique

of the work as a whole is the story "John the Baptist." It tells
of Karl Loer, who, like Frank before his mystical experience, has
no spiritual roots and is unhappy at the lack. He asks his Negro
cleaning woman why she is happy; she has orthodox religion
to put meaning in her life, and she advises him to pray. He
replies that he doesn't know whom to pray to. He sees a husband
and wife in the street, and clamped tightly across the wife's
breast he thinks he sees an iron bar, a symbol both of the barrenness of the life about him and the restrictions that were
all that religion meant to his parents. He is a professional
musician, and constantly has the ugliness of the commercial
associated with his art, which would otherwise be his salvation.
Books offer him no solution, even the psychologists cannot
help. Then he goes to the park and sees a grotesquely divergent
group of people: an idiot boy and a well-coordinated one, playing ball together; a dirty, blackbearded man who eats refuse;
a white-faced man who is constantly picking up scraps of paper,
reading them, and discarding them: and a Negro dwarf with a
huge head. Karl sits on a park bench, and beside him appears
a blond-bearded tramp, in whose presence all the others come
and introduce themselves to Karl and join in a dance in which
the park, the river, and the sky move, until Karl, urged to an
effort of will by the tramp, puts them all back as they were.
Turning to the tramp, Karl asks who he is. "What did it seem
to you, I was?" the tramp replies. "The first time that I saw
you," Karl says, "I said to myself: 'He looks like a ridiculous
Jesus!'". . .

" 'You were right in what you said to yourself,' he spoke.
'For I am John the Baptist.' "

This story is symbolic of Waldo Frank's own experience, in
which the one-ness of all things became known to him, the One
—God—becoming associated with reality. All things were joined,
and then went back to their respective places. This vision does
not represent pantheism, else they would not go back to their

places. Waldo Frank's philosophy does not include being able, except in moments of mystic enlightenment, to be conscious of the Whole alone: "To be conscious of the Whole is to live in terms of the Whole expressed through its parts."

Just as a knowledge of Frank's experience is a key to the meaning of the story, the story is a key to the novel—not an explanation of the novel, but one means by which its deeper meaning can be got at. For their meaning, the stories must be read; because their meaning, like that of any work of art, can be expressed only in them. The city block has spread out to enclose the world, yet it remains a city block. When Mrs. Lipper has sexual intercourse with Father Dennis she is receiving the sacrament from him, but their act remains carnal, sin and sacrament at the same time. The people in the novel often do the wrong things, but if they do them for the right motives, they find redemption.

Clarence Lipper, in the opening story, "Accolade," sets out from work with six dollars in his pocket to buy his wife an ivory comb-and-brush. "She had made hints. She was at home this moment, primed to be surprised at the brush-and-comb of celluloid 'tortoise shell' which Clarence was to bring her." But he meets a friend who invites him to come for a drink—to wish him a merry Christmas. He refuses:

"Can't be done." ... The sky cracked open.
Like a little red bird came
a brightness
downward.
It grew. Below the sky, over the blind multitude, came Jesus . . . gracefully afloat with one hand forward. He wore a scarlet robe and a gold crown; he wore sandals. He was dressed like the Christ in the Altar of Clarence Lipper's church. He wafted downward as on a gentle sea: one hand in advance like a prow. Very softly with his forefinger he touched the pursed firm lips of Clarence. He disappeared. The crack in the sky was gone.

Clarence Lipper was large. The crowds of the City, shopping, shrank. But he stood pendulous before his friend. His arm swung loose. There was a wonderful thirst in his mouth.

Daley locked an arm in the arm of Clarence. They marched off, humming two tunes.

The money for the present reduced from the price of the ivory to the price of the celluloid, and he not even drunk, he goes to another bar, and after that dumps his remaining change in the box of a street-corner peddler. He will give his wife a really Christian present: the power to see him clearly. But on the way home he knocks into Mrs. Luve (in a later story we learn she is mistress of a house of assignation), who invites him in for a drink. She seems broken, miserable, and his warmth toward her leads him to accept. Sitting with her, three doors from his own wife, he is overcome with despondency, breaks down, and tells what he has done. She gives him a silver comb-and-brush, to give to his wife.

"Now, go home. Quick. Say anything you like." She studied him. "Better say nothing. Let her think you were delayed . . . let her forget to think with looking at her gift."

The box was in his hands: his hat and his coat also.

"I don't understand," he rebelled.

She smiled . . . dim eyes suddenly bright and filling a dim face. Then she was serious.

"This is Christmas Eve," was her answer. Impalpably, she pressed him to the door.

A continuity, both in the book and in the relations of persons with one another, is suggested by having the characters of some stories become symbols in others. Mrs. Luve is only symbol; she has no story to herself in *City Block*, although Frank sketched one out in his notebook. Activator of the greater reward of Clarence Lipper, who went out to buy ivory, wasted until he could not buy celluloid, but ended up with silver, giver of the accolade, she serves also in the story "Faith" as the redeemer of a pair of clandestine lovers. Rudd, who loses his wife and finally comes to accept life without her, and Godfrey Carber, who is in love with his wife's youth, together turn up as provokers of desire in the lovers of "Journey's End," who at first are attracted to each other only as a means of filling the emptiness they become aware of in their lives by observing Rudd and Carber. The Lanichs and the Rabinowiches turn up in each other's stories, each couple having what the other envies: the Lanichs a sound child, and the Rabinowiches a tawdry prosperity. As presences, all the characters form an occasionally-visible human background in all the stories, making a continuum from which, it seems, the author has snipped only enough portions that we can sense the shape of it all, selecting the parts which are symbols of the whole as it is done in poetry, rather than making what Beach, in *The Twentieth Century Novel*, calls a breadthwise or lengthwise cutting.

City Block becomes so personal that it can be highly offensive to many readers. Sex to Frank *is* a sacrament; indeed it is in the Christian religion as it was in those religions from which Christianity derived, but society has come to expect men and women not to treat sex as something holy, so that the nature of the taboo has become confused. To Frank miracles, Christs, and John the Baptists seem as possible in the Twentieth Century as in the First, and the ordinary man's inability to believe this, turning them into distortions and negations of their reality, he finds ridiculous. Thus it is he can make a figure of humor of Christ, when Christ is the Christmas spirit that makes a man get drunk.

In the final analysis taste is the subject matter of anthropology. It is a result of culture in the individual, and when a thing is judged as attractive or repulsive alone, disregarding its truth or falsehood, it productiveness or barrenness, the judgment is based only on the common denominator of totems and taboos in the culture in which it is judged. Insofar as that statement is true, Waldo Frank is a man without taste: he sees a thing, not as an entity, but in terms of its purpose, its motives, and the values concerned. In the *City Block* story "—And Charity," a father who had deserted his wife and infant seeks out the child when she is seventeen years old, her mother dead five years. She had gone to an orphanage for three years after her mother's death, and since then has been a shopgirl. Without telling her who he is, he takes her to dinner and goes to her room to talk of her mother. As he talks, he covers up his remorse, his sorrow and love for her, by disparaging her father, whom, he tells her, he met after the desertion. He speaks of her father as dead, as damned, and when she becomes aware of who he is, she leads him to possess her. With our taboo on incest (a universal taboo among mankind, one must confess, but disregarded by the animals) we are shocked. The act seems particularly distasteful because she provokes it. But the *purpose* of her act is a sacrifice which, if loss of virginity is a "fate worse than death," should make her a saint. Not revealing that she knows who he is, she gives him completely of her love. The purity of her motive is the virtue named in the title of the story—*caritas*; the purity of Frank's motive in the story is clear.

The purity of his motive in "Ecclesia Sanctae Teresae" would be questioned by the orthodox. It is not for nothing that the church of Father Luis Ájala Dennis is named for St. Theresa. Father Dennis is a young man with a sound body. His vocation seems to have resulted from an incestuous desire for his mother, accompanied by the wish, in denying it, to deny also her ambitions for him: to grow rich, to marry a rich girl. From the elevated he sees the people in the street as possessors of a secret that he is outside; he is beset with religious doubts, does not pray, does not read his breviary. Awaiting him outside his room above the church is Mr. Kandro. Like the priest, Mr. Kandro has never had sexual intercourse; he is sixty-five years

old and believes he now never will. Yet he is full of desire, and
wants the priest to advise him, while he plays devil's advocate.
He wants to know what the priest, who must keep his chastity,
does when desire comes on him. In anguish for the same reason,
Father Dennis sees himself at sixty-five with the same guilty
feeling of barrenness as Mr. Kandro, and is stung by Mr. Kandro's penetrating: "A woman's body is a white straight thing.
It is a healing we can take upon us. . . . Is it Pride and the love
of your Hurt that keeps you also away from the white healing?"

Mr. Kandro leaves, and Father Dennis sinks down before
the crucifix on the wall in confusion at this argument, until
Mrs. Lipper comes. She feels an inadequacy in herself as a wife,
something symbolized by her having been inexperienced before
marriage and feeling that in love she is only taker, never giver.
As she stands before him, he thinks, "What is Sin but a lack,
a great Hunger?" They have intercourse, and she, in leaving,
says, "I have something now to give at last to my husband."
Father Dennis too feels purer, feels exultant. His spirit dances,
and the world swings up and down: "calm swinging. Jerusalem
packed with prayer, Rome red with argument . . ." The sensa-
tion of the act with Mrs. Lipper fades, and he feels he must
retain it—because it is the healing of his hurt, and because it
will enable him to live as a priest. For the power to retain it
he thinks of his Church: "And like a frightened boy, he rushed
praying down stairs. . . ."

This is a definite identification of sexual abstinence with sin,
and an attack on the confusion between puritanism and purity.
It is intolerant of the rules of the Catholic Church, although
it is positive in its approval of the spirit of Christianity, and, I
believe, especially Catholicism. The statue of Christ in Father
Dennis's room has, however, no hands, and since Mr. Kandro's
hands are red, the symbol of murder, and barrenness is identified with murder in the story "Murder," it would seem that

Frank is saying that Christ is red-handed, and the Church has cut off his hands to conceal them. Concealment is in the symbol of the handless Christ, at any rate, referred to also in *Rahab*.

Any identification of Mr. Kandro's red hands with masturbation would be uncalled for; Frank does not use obvious erotic symbols of a platitudinous sort, nor is he interested in the physiology of sin. It is this very thing—his implication that sin is a state of being rather than an act—that justifies his material in the story. Mrs. Lipper's inadequacy could be biologically explained as clitoral—incomplete—orgasm or frigidity; but to emphasize the physical would mean to lose the point of Frank's writing. His symbols do not stand for things, or they would be symbols only for obscurity's sake, and since his symbols refer to spiritual states that can be communicated only through symbolism, it is proper that he challenge the distortion he finds in worldly or barren uses of the symbolism of the Judeo-Christian tradition. Obviously "Ecclesia Sanctae Teresae" is not an empty attack on clerical chastity. Strictly speaking, it attacks nothing, but values religion that is expressed through the whole being and not just through the mind. Constant reiteration of the word "think" by the priest as he resists what his whole self considers right indicates that he is trying to act only through his mind. By his failure he has come closer to St. Theresa.

City Block is not a riddle. It is subjective, and its full meaning emerges only through creative reading and re-reading of the work as a whole, but no obstacles are put in for the puzzle's sake, nor is there deliberate ambiguity. Indeed, the book is perfectly clear on the surface, and the statements and actions can be taken at face value. The farther the reader probes beneath the surface, however, the more complex the book becomes. The structure is simple: a series of episodes in the lives of people who live in the same block, showing something of the currents and counter-currents in their lives, the relations of one to another, suggesting the continuum of which all their lives are a part.

The suggestion of the Whole is best illustrated by the story most evasive to the critics: the last one, "Beginning." Paolo Benati says:

I gave these stories to the man that wrote them. It was hard. Many times after I had reached him I lost him. I was not alone in trying to hold him. When I was moved to give my stories to him, I did not think that others might demand him. I began leisurely, nameless. He had no thought of me, no belief in my being. He had enormous belief in his own. So my will weakened toward him. I became pale, a ghost in my need of giving these stories.

At last I found him rightly. He was in great anguish. He believed, so serious a displacement had followed so vast a flood of conflict, that he was destroyed in spirit. He said to himself: "I am a failure. I am of those sacrificed and consumed." I waited. He said: "I accept this. I am a failure. So be it. I have no claim on other than my fate. So be it. . . . There is no injustice," I heard him say, "there is God."

Then I seized him. "Go away," I said, "into some quiet. I have much to say to you. I am a boy and from your standpoint dead. Perhaps you are what you call a failure. Let me use you, since it is good so. I can promise nothing, save that I want you."

He gave to my urgency upon him. I held him tortured, in obedience. It was good to see him at my work: on a train, at odd hours of the night, in a room filled with the green tumult of drunken sailors. . . . At all times he was an instrument I used . . . gradually wearing out, bleeding away . . . but a good tool.

And so, now that I have delivered myself through him, I release him. I tell about myself, place myself where I belong among these lives that have borne me: and let him go. For there are others not done with him: one in especial I see, greater than I, far better and far greater: with dark hot old eyes . . . my own are young . . . one whose breast is high with Song as the trunk of a great tree, whose mouth is heavy with Prayer as a vine with ripe grapes. This one approaches to make his voice, already heard at times, unintermittent, Whole. He is high but he is kind. For he has paused, looking upon me with a sweet forbearance, until I have done with my scribe . . .

This passage contains, of course, many kinds of symbolism. Paolo Benati, at the simplest level, is the conception of the book; he is the materials, the people, the life-force of the block on the East Side, between Seventy-seventh and Seventy-eighth Streets, east of Avenue A, that clamored for expression in Waldo Frank's unconscious; he is the associative power of the un-conscious—but aside from this symbolism, this is a literal state-ment of the creation of the book; the other side of the coin that, on one side, is "John the Baptist." The "man that wrote" these stories is Waldo Frank; the "I" his religious creative consciousness, the Jesus who was baptized by the blond-bearded tramp. The "one greater than I" can refer to God, to the Jews, or, more particularly, may refer to Frank's plan to write a book called "Sabbatai Zevi." "Beginning" and "John the Baptist" together make the genesis of City Block, for the mystical ex-perience had its outlet through the social experience of living on an East Side block very remote from the regimented middle class neighborhood of Waldo Frank's childhood.

Paolo Benati tells us, as his story continues, that he is an Italian immigrant boy, his father a cheerful, successful barber, his mother sensitive but ugly. Paolo never smiles; at first fears that the stone building will smash the fragile-looking glass-fronted shop of his father; when he conquers his fear of entering the shop, he becomes the shoeshine boy. Money, ambition, he rejects; he is content to shine shoes, to dream. Although the other characters in the book express themselves through action, he expresses himself through inaction, in watching, hearing voices, having visions. At the age of fifteen he buys a pistol and shoots himself.

This story is the other side of still another coin. Inadequacy in *City Block* is spiritual inadequacy. The Lanichs in "Under the Dome—aleph" have all the ingredients of happiness but the power to see that they do. Paolo Benati has nothing but spirit. With no life outside the spiritual, he is dead, and his suicide is only an admission that he is dead. Here we have retained some of the old irony of Waldo Frank, but it is irony that has undergone great change; it is creative. It balances the previous stories, modifying "develop your spirit" into "be whole!" Paolo's only action is his haunting of the writer, to express himself through his stories—after his death. The analogy to Christ is obvious, and the death at fifteen, half Jesus's age at the crucifixion, may be significant. The center of the book, after all, is John the Baptist; this is the book of the forerunner of the messiah. It delves deeply into life, but at the appearance of death, it stops. Death comes to seven characters: the babies in "Murder," Rudd's wife in "The Table," a nameless white man in "Hope," Dora in "Candles," and Lathran in "The Altar of the World." In "Candles" and "The Table," attention is centered on the living and what loss teaches them; in "Hope" and "The Altar of the World" methods of facing death are shown. None of the stories make any attempt at interpretation of death; thus "Beginning" gives us a half-Jesus (although the analogy should not be strained, as in the story it is not) whose book is about unity in life. It took Waldo Frank thirty more years, using story materials he had already begun to accumulate, to go beyond this limitation he had set for *City Block*. In the meantime one of his *City Block* characters was to lead him to another phase of the lyric novel, and he would evolve, after preparation through social action, a means of integrating society in the foreground of his fiction.

7

Rahab

OF THE FOURTEEN STORIES ORIGINALLY PLANNED FOR *City Block* according to the outline of 1916, in Notebook VI, only seven eventually appeared as part of the book. Two of the four written by the time the outline was made, "Delicatessen" and "Bread-Crumbs," were dropped from the plan, although the latter was published in the *Seven Arts* in 1917. Five more were planned and never written, but two of these, at least, provided background characters for the stories that are part of *City Block*. One of them, never titled, was planned as the story of the Negro cleaning woman who tries to console Karl Loer with her faith in "John the Baptist." The other, entitled "The Bad Woman" in the outline, was sketched in the following note:

Theme for Story

The real genesis of a bad woman. How she turns her weakness into effectiveness, by crushing out heart, love, sentiment, honor, service—and when her pride is gone, she crumbles.

From girlhood—.

This is quite a different creature from the Fanny Luve who bestows the accolade on Clarence Lipper and is the salvation of the policeman and the nursemaid who rent a room from her for their clandestine meetings. Fanny Luve obviously grew from *City Block*, rather than from the story Frank originally had in mind. She does not act in the rôle of prostitute in these stories,

76

but as a woman who, because she is outside any social order in the block, can be a critic and a setter-off of reactions. It is evident, however, at her first appearance that she is an outcast. She is "drab and battered, a miserable woman. She wore no hat upon her arid hair, a black shawl fended her throat. He knew what she was." According to the old cliché, every whore is supposed to have had an unusual background, and to have turned to the streets as a result of some dramatic betrayal, disappointment in love, or unforgivable sin. All vestiges of this stereotype are present in the *City Block* stories where she appears. In "Accolade" she has an expensive brush-and-comb of silver, not used for over twenty years, indicating that she had come down in the world but cherished her memories. In "Faith," her having been "broken" by the police is referred to by the policeman, Patrick Broaddus. When she confronts the nursemaid she tells her that she has known what love is, and "what horror comes, when love is starved or denied." The same story is implied, plus a comedown in her own profession. The story that was to be Frank's next novel was already taking form.

These stories were completed in March, 1920. In April, Frank wrote Part I of *Rahab*, probably intending it too to be a part of *City Block*, but, without doubt, discovering that it was developing into a story of larger scope than the others. He returned to *The Dark Mother* next, making the final revision and sending it to the printer, and until August worked on materials for his proposed book on Jewish themes; then returning to *Rahab*, wrote Parts Two, Three, and Seven in August, October, and November, respectively. In the first two months of 1921 he was travelling through the South, and on his return to New York wrote the Foreword to the German edition of *Our America* and an essay, "The American Year," that appeared in the Munich *Neue Merkur* (June, 1921) and the *Nouvelle Revue Française* (September, 1921), but not working on any fiction. In June he sailed for Portugal and Spain, and began collecting the impressions that were to make *Virgin Spain*. By September he was in Paris, finishing two of the last stories for *City Block*, and then *Rahab*. On his return to New York, *Rahab* was sent to the printer. It was published in March, 1922, while revision was continued on some of the stories in *City Block*, "Candles" being entirely rewritten, and "Ecclesia Sanctae Teresae" done for the first time. The delay in publishing *City Block* was not just because the book was not ready; it could have been published, although it was improved by the changes made in the time afforded by the delay. The reason for delay was practical rather than esthetic; there was a "book purity" movement afoot under John Sumner, of the New York Society for the Prevention of Vice, that made publication of the novel risky. After some consideration, Frank decided to publish the book himself, rather than have Boni and Liveright take the risks of commercial publication (which they were rather reluctant to do anyway), issuing it in a limited edition of 1,250 copies from his home in Darien, Connecticut, in September, 1922. It did not appear in a trade edition until 1929, when Scribner's was Frank's publisher and the problem of censorship had abated.

Thus it was that although *City Block* was the source of *Rahab*, *Rahab* appeared first. The only critic of Frank who has seemed to be aware of the correct sequence is Gorham Munson, and even so, he treats *Rahab* first in his remarkably perceptive *Waldo Frank: A Study*. Since *Holiday* had not been written by the time Munson's book appeared, no great harm was done by the reversal; but the perpetuation of the incorrect sequence in subsequent studies has prevented critics from seeing what kind of transition was made between *City Block* and *Holiday*.

The flaws in *Rahab* are inherent in its growth away from the *City Block* episodic structure to the lyrical entity of *Holiday*. Originally intended as a short story, the theme proved to be too worthy of development to be left as such, and it did not fit the completed cycle. The first two parts of the story, Fanny's marriage and her separation from her husband, were written before the final revision of *City Block*, and they, except for the frame that was added later, have the flaws of Frank's apprentice work. In Part Four, written in Paris in 1921 the shift occurs; the portion before Fanny's mystical experience, largely set in a flashback within a flashback, is the technique of a story like "Rudd," but not conclusive, as an episode in that technique must be. Its material, the downfall of Fanny to the edge of the gutter, is to the manner of *City Block* as a sonnet without the sestet would be to a whole one. But from the mystical experience on, almost the entire second half of the novel, the technique of the second phase of the lyrical novel is used, with episodes that, employing a variety of effects, work up on a larger scale to a climactic scene, rather than using the smaller-scale device of a series of scenes working up to a climactic moment.

What Frank needed was a large-scale central episode adaptable to his method and his theme, and once he became aware of the need, the episode was there waiting. In his year of reporting for the *Post* and the *Times*, he had not only mingled with a variety of New Yorkers, but in his daily work got a reporter's-eye view of the city and its people. At the height of the summer heat of 1912, a crime was committed that implicated nearly the whole police force and was played to the hilt by all the newspapers. Herman Rosenthal, a gambler who had recently moved his establishment uptown to 104 West Forty-fifth Street, competing with the uptown gambling elite, had been operating in partnership with Lieutenant Charles Becker, of the Strong Arm Squad, for the sake of protection, but the uptown gambling fraternity had more powerful protection, so Becker raided Rosenthal on April 15. A police guard was put over Rosenthal, but on July 11 he evaded his guard and went to the District Attorney and in a sworn statement revealed the whole protection setup. The New York *World* gave the exposé headlines, although most of the other papers buried it. On July

16, 1912, at 2:00 A.M., Rosenthal was called from his late supper at the Hotel Metropole, on Forty-third Street near Times Square, and as he reached the sidewalk, six loiterers stopped lounging about and began shooting. They sped off in a large gray car, and the one policeman on the scene had trouble finding a cab to give chase, and lost the murder car in a few blocks. It later came out that the police had cleared the cabs from the vicinity some time before the murder, to make pursuit difficult. The Rosenthal murder dominated the news for over a month, the *World* driving the authorities to an investigation that eventually revealed Becker as the man who "ordered" the murder, and Big Jack Zelig and five other Jewish gunmen as the loiterers. Zelig himself was murdered before he could testify, but the public was indignant, not only over the corruption among the police, but, spurred by the clear identification of the murderers as Jews (although Becker was not), considerable anti-Jewish feeling arose.

This case would have lasted in Waldo Frank's memory, not only because he, as a reporter, interviewed the principals, but because of the Jewish aspect of the case, and the fact that the police commissioner, who defended his men just a bit longer than he should have, was Commissioner Waldo. Many interesting incidental characters appeared, and some of these had a part in creating the characters of *Rahab*. The mistress of one of the murderers, a woman who went by the name of Rose Harris sometimes, and sometimes called herself Regina Gordon, tickled the imaginations of the reporters, although she had no part in the crime. Mrs. Rosenthal, hidden by her veil, went in and out of the Municipal Building and was reluctant to talk to reporters to just the right dramatic degree. These fascinating people, and the dramatic events, provided a basis from which Waldo Frank, in Paris nine years later, was able to construct the ultimate downfall of Fanny Luve.

It was in Paris also that the atmosphere-building device of

the frame was incorporated into the story. All of Fanny's life
is told in flashbacks of memory while she sits drinking wine
and talking with Samson Brenner, a young Jew who is waiting
for the return of one of Fanny's "girls," then out at a show.
In the beginning Fanny answers the door, leaving the chain
hooked while she sees who is calling. She is obviously lonely
and apprehensive.

> The door opened against the drawn chain, grating against it.
> In the grey strip a woman's face, very grey, very unexpectant,
> suddenly was bright.
> It measured a man, young, standing at ease. The chain clicked
> free. "O it's you, Mr. Samson." The door opened wide, shut them
> in. The hall was a long shadow beyond the glow of them standing.
> He was quiet waiting, not sheer against her: his shaggy coat poured
> the street's coldness. She was a dim thing about eyes.
> "I'm so glad it's you, Mr. Samson."
> She walked noiseless through shadow, she took no space from it,
> she was infinitesimal within a mood. He followed.
> "I was taking it right easy . . . reading."

While they talk, they think; the talk is recorded conventionally with the use of quotation marks, and unspoken thoughts
are preceded by a dash, as conversation is punctuated in French.
He is repelled and attracted by her, and decides to wait for
the return of the girl he wants. She gets out wine, and as his
thoughts become more intense, they are presented as verse. As
they talk, the flashbacks begin, first just in bits, as her memories;
then with the frame episodes being spaced wider apart and finally stopping, making an unconscious transition, as Fanny might
make between remembering her past and telling the story of her
life to her visitor. Toward the end, the frame episodes appear
again, with dialogue to show that Fanny has been telling about
her life. The book ends with the return of Samson's girl and
his going to her room with her.
The background material about Fanny, the first half of her

story, is as psychologically sound and artistically unmotivated as the childhood of the unwelcome man. Although there are passages that are as powerful with subjective emotion as any in *City Block*, and although the figures of Fanny's husband, her lover, and the people in New York are as vivid as the secondary characters in *The Dark Mother*, the total conception seems labored. Even the clashing irony of *The Dark Mother* comes again, with details and commonplace dialogue detracting from the guilt that grows within Fanny, in itself a powerful accumulation of foreboding. This development, remarkable in conception, but really not a part of the rest of the book, is obviously vestige of the Ur-Rahab. "The real genesis of a bad woman. How she turns her weakness into effectiveness by crushing out heart, love, sentiment, honor, service—and when her pride is gone, she crumbles. From girlhood—."

The story begins with Fanny being seduced by Harry Luve. They are Southerners; Harry is the son of wealthy parents, and Fanny obviously comes from the same class. She waits until he is done with college, and then they are married. Their love seems idyllic, but he has begun drinking in college, and he gets worse. While she is pregnant, he goes on an extended binge, returning two years later, reformed by an evangelist. In the meantime, she has had an affair with a Jewish lawyer from Washington who was in town on a case, and when she tells Harry, who has returned more sanctimonious than contrite, he quotes, "whosoever shall put away his wife saving for the cause of fornication causeth her to commit adultery," and sends her away. She considers suicide, but decides to live, and leaves Virginia for the North. In Washington she visits her former lover, who tells her that now she must live for herself, forgetting her child, whom she left with her husband. "Clear feet carried body erect through the stone city. Mother worlds in blood poured from her, leaving white feet, white body, while the soul of Fanny swooned in a ruthless knowledge."

In the portion told like part of a *City Block* story, Fanny, on an autumn walk with Christopher Johns, whose mistress she has become, remembers her coming to New York and starting work in the office of Johns's soft-drink factory. She recalls the room she took and her friendship with a co-worker, Clara Lonergan. Her growing feeling of guilt is developed, motivating the compulsion to go downward which continues through the remaining portion of the first half of her story. She leaves Johns, works as a factory hand, goes into the streets, sinks into poverty. Downward she goes, until in her sordid room, huddling over a kerosene heater in the depth of winter, she comes to a mystical feeling of being again without guilt.

Not only does this mark a turning point in the life of Fanny; the story itself shifts gears here. She thinks that she senses a pattern of Jews in her life:

—On Broadway there are women with burnt souls, and there are Jews. New York is full of Jews. What does that mean? Spirit of a Jew quenched the white-stockinged girl: bore her to womanhood. Word of a Jew thrust her forth. Hand of a Jew guided me to this Cold seeking warmth . . . led me to this City where there are Jews in swarms, in sultry pools, in tumults!

She argues with God, ending without her sense of prevading guilt, and sleeps soundly. She awakens hungry, and bathes with a feeling of baptism. She has only a nickel, and goes to a bake-shop to buy rolls. The woman scrubbing the floor there gives her a hot meal, and she goes out, rediscovering the world:

Street! —why does no thing stay as it was? So I can catch up?
She breathed heavily. Her head was light, save in the very back under the coiled hair which tipped downward pulling up her chin. She felt her stomach. Her knees were light. She felt her feet. —I could laugh! I am striped in heaviness and lightness. Laugh then!
The two walls of the street fell forward: in the air above the gutter they crashed in silence together and disappeared. The City was

a maze of twisting streams. . . . Two men passed. They were arm in arm. They were sleek and full in the black coats shaped to their bodies. Their cheeks and their eyes were sleek and full of themselves. About the round head of each there was an Aura. Thick troubled, it beat outward like an emprisoned gas. A gaseous colorless world it was about the head of each, that veered against the other, drew in, thrust out, hostile. Impenetrable two men passed, arm in arm.

Although Fanny finds work again, in the shop of a fur-dresser, she is taken ill shortly after, and lies alone in her shabby room. Eventually Clara, her friend from Johns's establishment, finds her, and takes her home to what is apparently a room provided by Johns, whose mistress Clara now is. During Fanny's convalescence, two more kept women visit; Clara later tells the story of one of them, and that harlot's progress is a very effective tale. The child of an orthodox Jew who keeps a small store in a little Carolina town, Tess showed an early aptitude for music, and was trained on the violin. When she was ready to go to New York to prepare for a concert career, her father mortgaged the store and sold his most cherished possession—really his only valuable possession—a piece of Jewish ritual jewelry, in order to send her. But she learned that her hands were not big enough for concert playing. Clara tells:

". . . Well, Tessie hadn't come to New York and put the Liebovitz clan on bread and water and made the old man sell part of his religion for another part, just to play fiddle in a restaurant. She went to a doctor or something of the sort who told her he could stretch her fingers. He stretched 'em alright—"

Fanny raised herself on her arms from the pillow, her eyes still shut.

"—till something tore."

"Till something broke."

"It was all over."

"I know the rest," said Fanny. . . .

They finally decide to take a house together, all four. Susan's man, a police lieutenant named Statt, in charge of the Strong Arm Squad, that raids gamblers and houses of ill-fame, and Tess's, Abraham Mangel, the owner of a gambling house, are friends—indeed, business associates—the lieutenant getting a large portion of his income from Mangel. Clara's is a judge. They are successful and happy in their house, although the climax suggested by the Rosenthal murder is suggested when, on their first evening there, Statt brings a case of champagne from a house of prostitution he has raided, because the owner haggled over her protection money. He later refers to having raised the price on Mangel. Still, Fanny seems to add something to all their lives. To Mangel's she adds too much. As they sit in silence, their thoughts are given in the form of verse. Mangel thinks:

—Tessie should be my daughter.
   Then the fear of God would keep her flesh away.
   You have shown me, Luve woman, that Tessie is my
      daughter.

—I am made of filth. If I could stop hating myself!
   I am a dirty Jew. . . I hate Statt. . . He makes me feel—
    this. . .
   But who is he?
   His body is straighter because he has no soul.
   (There are times when I would love to kiss his body.)

—My soul is beautiful. My soul says to me:
   You are a dirty Jew! . . .
   What is the use? One picks the smut from one's nose,
   But one's nose smells on, the smut comes back,
   What is the use of having a beautiful soul?
   No one tells Statt that he is a dirty Dutchman.

—You, little girl, with the apple breasts and the hips
   hard and sweet like an apple,

> You are my soul and you are far away.
> You should be my daughter.
> Then I should not have to hold you naked. . .
> She is my daughter! O if I could say that, say:
>   Father!
> Not: —a whore and a dirty Jew that keeps her.

After six years of the house, Mangel's conscience overpowers him; he has one of his own places raided. He makes an appointment with the District Attorney to betray the whole system. Fanny refuses to permit Statt to have Mangel killed in her house, so after he is killed elsewhere, the police raid Fanny's. The group is broken up, Clara dies in the prison hospital of an illness she was suffering when she was picked up, and Fanny comes eventually to where we found her at the opening of the novel, madame of an ordinary house.

At no point in the later progress of Fanny do we lose interest or have a doubt. Every action is both natural and symbolic. The purity of Fanny, her unwillingness to betray, her power to evoke the best in people—these things are thoroughly motivated. Each of the characters is distinct, complex, and real. The cold squeezing out and sordid murder of a gambler is transformed into a symbolic act with its drama being enhanced rather than reduced. And with the denouement, the thorough symbolism of Fanny's destroying herself to keep from betraying Mangel is made ironically clear. She has told this touching story to another Jew, another person, young, but very sensitive, who should have understood the spiritual wholeness that was in that act. They sit silent, until the return of the girl he has come for:

> Fanny heard the door shut. She was alone. She sat down where she had sat before at the table. She arose. She shut out the gas. A peal of Thelma's laughter pierced the door. The room clapped close about the fainting flame of the one candle.
> Fanny sat down where she had sat before. Beyond the empty

place was the Night. Within her gaze was the Night. Her eyes held
nothing.

"And a Jew," she murmured "a Jew was to bring me Light."

. . .

"—and God?"

Sudden her eyes were hard. "Think of him," she spoke. Her
mouth full of tears made her voice liquid. "Think of him, Fanny.
No one else! . . Your Light-bearer, your Prophet, your Voice in the
Wilderness—there he is, out there, in the arms of Thelma. . .
Fanny, dare to think."

The title *Rahab*, referring to the prostitute who hid the
Jewish spies in the city of the Philistines, makes a key to the
pattern of the story. The original Rahab, we can imagine, gained
spiritually from her dangerous act. The Bible makes no mention
of her being rewarded, although it says she was "saved alive"
after the fall of the city. Fanny, whose life too hinged on the
actions of Jews, came to her worldly downfall for the sake of
a Jew whom she would not betray—Mangel. And she like Rahab,
gained, not from earthly reward for her act, not from gratitude
from those she put herself in jeopardy for—indeed, she is a
Rahab whose Jew lost the city—not, it is safe to say, from a
reward in heaven, but from a spiritual gain inherent in the act.
That is the source of all the greatness of soul in Fanny, from
the beginning of her history. A prideful Fanny died as a result
of the adversities and guilt-drive of the first part; a soulful Fanny
grew through adversity, taking the place of the Fanny who died.

The death-and-birth motif was in time to be pursued further
by Frank. The transition from the story-cycle to the novel with
a single lyrical sweep—for transition is what *Rahab* is—was to be
completed before the end of two years.

8

Holiday

TWO PAGES PAST THE RECORD OF THE MYSTICAL EXPERIENCE OF
February 28, 1920, in Notebook VII is the following item:

Story   CARNIVAL
Here's a Magnificent Theme for Your Hand—

A study of life in a small Mississippi town—the dearth of outlet,
the constant, terrible petty repressiveness, the falsity of the preach-
ing, the cheat of the 'movies'—the gradual growth of the hidden
passionate tumor—and its inevitable outbreak in 1) the negro's
raping a girl and 2) the whole community's lynching of the negroes.
Holiday. Festival. Carnival.

Juxtaposed: The ugly huddled 'white' town of frame houses, tin-
front bank & P.O. trees cut down: white wood churches & the
niggertown—hinterland of sparse pine, live oak, yupon, gray grass,
& paintless shanties.

HOLIDAY

Opening: The sun, reddening, levelling, falling, thro high thin
pines: the woods full of copper green glints & song & laughter:
Everywhere negroes and children calling, shouting. The determined gang of muttering whites, hear the music: it seems to mock
them: pass occasional girls or boys—silent—music everywhere else:
girls' [loneliness? loveliness?] marks them too. The downtrodden
people, living in song & pinetrees: & the maddened, deprived mas-

ters. The colored song they cannot touch, any more than they can the colored sunset. . . .

Some town on the Gulf, seen while Frank was travelling in Louisiana, Mississippi, and Alabama late in 1920, inspired that note. From June to December, 1922, he was in Darien, Connecticut, save for a short trip South with Jean Toomer, the Negro writer, in September, a sort of field trip, and in November the book was in first draft. Revision took place early the next year, and in March, *Holiday* went to the printer.

Although written just as rapidly, and revised almost as rapidly, *Holiday* does not suffer as *Rahab* does from being created by a writer in rapid transition. For one thing, Frank was kept in Darien by the problems of publishing *City Block*, and it is possible that the domesticity resulting from the birth of his first child, Thomas, on May 12, 1922, had a settling effect on him. In addition, acclaim was beginning to come from abroad. Lise Landau was preparing to translate his books into German, and French translations were being planned. Frank had already decided to write *Virgin Spain* and was making arrangements for his tour and studying Spanish intensively. He was riding the top of the wave, his notebooks showing more and more ambitious plans. On November 5, 1922, he recorded completion of the rough draft of *Holiday* and in the same entry envisioned three volumes of sequel to *The Dark Mother!* He considered a book to be called "The Godless Ghetto," which he had had in the back of his mind for twelve years, but because the themes had changed shape, decided against it. He proposed three plays, one of which he was to write before the end of two years. He considered again the book on French literature which had grown out of his Yale work. This was a time of planning rather than of internal revolution; recognition, even fame, seemed inevitable. Above all else, he had found, in the latter half of *Rahab*, the form which suited his purpose.

Holiday is the peak of the lyrical novel impulse in Frank's development. The creative use of irony that began in *City Block* —the use of irony, not as a comment on a situation, but as the central concept from which a story is developed—grew to encompass an entire novel. The irony of John Cloud's being lynched for a crime he did not commit—being lynched as a result of his virtue—is integral, not just to the story, but to the whole conception of *Holiday*. Contrary to their usual symbolic content, black is good and white is evil; yet this is more than a simple reversal. Black is earth, the solid, the whole, and white is a ghost, dim, false. It is not the conventional world turned upside down, but an entirely new world.

Holiday is no more a story about the South than Kafka's *Amerika* is a guide book. The religious symbolism evidencing this is almost too obvious: John Cloud's name associates with the sky—heaven—and his initials are J. C. Virginia, the white girl who plays Judas, and her evil brother and corrupt father are the Hades. The setting is Nazareth and its suburb, Niggertown. The symbolism, however, does not merely echo the passion of Christ, or even the struggle of good and evil between John and his people and Virginia and hers, but expresses the struggle for wholeness within John and within Virginia. On the surface, the flaws of the white world are very obvious; more subtly, the chief flaw of both worlds is incompleteness, a need for the other. Attempting as we have before to discuss the meaning of a work of art whose whole meaning can only be expressed by its own words, we can oversimplify and say that the black world is the material, the white the spiritual, conventionally expressed by religion. Our physical selves, Frank seems to be saying, are primitive, just evolving from the caveman; our spiritual structure is decadent. In these respects we are like the rural Southern Negro and the smalltown Southern White communities, living together but remaining separate. Each shuts the other out, yet they are interdependent.

It is the spiritual weakness of the black world that makes the lynching of John Cloud possible. Thus we see he is a reverse Christ—or a reverse of the conventional idea of Christ, whom we think of as being crucified by the worldly. In another sense, however, Christ, being substituted for Barabbas by the people of God, for daring to be a link between the worldly and the spiritual, has in his story a similar irony.

In its simplicity the world of *Holiday* seems almost to be the reality for which the conventional world is a confusing symbol. The intensity of the novel results from the development or a form almost perfectly suited to the subject matter. By degrees, Frank came to create characters that were less himself, while he, as storyteller, remained inside them. He stripped the expository from his writing, relying more and more on the suggestive power of words, until he gained the great economy of *Holiday*. He moved entirely outside the world he was born in, creating a new world as if from the symbols of the material world.

The feeling of a Southern small town is presented with striking vividness, for all that the story is not about the South in a naturalistic sense. Nazareth is probably not identifiable with any particular town, or even with a town in any particular area; but it has the essense that all Southern small towns have in common. The dialogue is presented with an astonishing sense of the rhythms of Southern and Negro speech. In the latter, Frank was aided by Jean Toomer. The conflict is heightened beyond the naturalistic by being made part of an organic turbulence that increases to fury as the book develops. Framework of conflict is that between the races. Attraction and repulsion between the sexes, particularly the attraction between opposites and the repulsion of likes, conflict between the productive and the non-productive, polarity in religion—all contribute to the race conflict. Unholy alliances, such as those between religious

fervor and sexual orgy, fear and hate, contribute to the outcome, as do the attitudes and ideas of all the characters.

Both atmosphere and the characterization of John are laid
surely and firmly in the first few pages:

> Sunset at Nazareth.
>
> Niggers go home through the copperglow of pines. Niggers sing
> home.
>
> White men stand lean in the doors of paintless houses. White
> men stand still.
>
> The waters of the bay go red to the blue Gulf where swims the
> bloody sun . . . sunset on Nazareth.
>
> The Reverend Dill of the White Church cries:
>
> "Air we gwine t' live up to our blessed holy name? Air we gwine
> t' play cards 'n' dance 'n' drink co'n likker: or air we gwine t'be true
> t' the sperrit of our Lo'd Jesus Christ . . . *hallelujah!* . . . he nebber
> shot no craps, he nebber looked with lust upon no woman."
>
> Nazareth. The Gulf of Mexico drains soil from her, blood red, to
> seas gray with moving. Moving seas of the world move athwart
> Nazareth standing . . . *niggers move, niggers sing* . . . a clot of crim-
> son clay. But the trees sway up. And a dark man's eyes peer through
> the corridor of pine and yupon, he scents the flood of camphor
> leaves in the Fall:
>
>> —When the year dies why does she stir?
>> When the year dies why does she sing?
>
> He is tall and slender. His height and slenderness is lithe. He is
> the color of dusk on the shadowed road he walks. White folk call
> him 'Lank.' They do not see how his height sings, they do not see
> how frail and hungry he is beside the pine. 'Big nigger' they see.

We begin to sense the personality within that tall frame
as he encounters a Negro girl:

> "Yo'-all late." he says.
> "An' ef—?"
> "Yo' Mammy, she'll be sayin': wha' yo'-all done in de dark?"

The girl's laughter, angular and strong, pierces up as her legs
prance.

"An' I'll say to Mammy: 'Ah been wid Lank John Cloud.' An'
Mammy, she'll stroke mah arm. She'll smile an' she'll say: 'O wid
John? Well, dotter, da's alright. Ef yo'-all been wid *John*.'"

Yet he is sensitive, restive too, and his mother knows it. She
tells him of his uncle who had to leave the South; she warns
him about being insufficiently servile, and encourages him to
marry Mary Cartier, one of his own sort, but whom he would
want to protect and thus be more careful. Even in lyrical tone
the speech pattern is retained:

"Didn' yo' hear dat song? It was a woman of ours. Didn' it fit
right perfect in de night? Don' the night lie homelike on our
town . . . ?"

"Niggertown."

"Yo' ought to see the night yonder on Main Street, Mammy.
Night's all broke up with jagged, ugly lights. Night's runnin' away
from Main Street, all de time. It's our night, Mammy, an' it's our
red lan'."

The sense of foreboding grows with the descriptive passage
of white Nazareth that begins the second chapter. But description is not all—the boat *Psyche* is docking, and a Negro deck-
hand slips between the boat and the pier. Although a man
in the bow holds the gap with a plank, the Negro drowns
with no one trying to rescue him, even though Bob Hade, a
champion swimmer, is watching. This incident brings into
clearer definition the contrasts between the white and black
worlds through the antagonism between them. The next two
chapters exploit this shock, the first a scene in the white church,
the second the sermon of the Negro preacher. In the sermon
itself, on the conversion of Paul, race strife subtly intrudes:

"Which will it be? Christ's beggin'. Christ, he ain't proud.
Christ, he ain't like yo'-all niggers. He done got spat on. He turned

de other cheek. Dey lynched him, Christ. He prayed fo' 'em. He come back: sayin' Saul, Saul, I loves you yet. He ain't proud, Church. Does you hear me? He's a-callin' you. An' so's de Devil." . . .

"Paul's a-walkin' de Damascus road. A-threatenin' blood and slaughter. Does yo' see him, Church?"

He walked, he walked. He was Paul. His voice was a strange song weaving his way on the Damascus road; and the immanence of mystery in his eye and the full hate behind him. The vaulting, beating breath of the hid multitude was the world about his way.

"He's a sinner. Like us. A-walkin' to Damascus. When he sets eyes on a Christian, Paul's eyes flash hate; Paul's hands dey strike de Christian. An' he's a walking de Damascus road, sent by de Devil. Proud! Stuck-up! His clothes is rich. He's got pull, alright, he Paul. He votes. He's a real white man, a-struttin' full o' hate."

With this bitter humor, the ominous atmosphere is broken, and the book shifts to the lyrical, John Cloud in bed, feeling that perhaps he will marry Mary, feeling good about his people and the land they are close to. But as he drifts toward sleep, portents of evil to come arise in him:

—Away from the warm swamp with your cabin flowers.
   Mammy, how wise you are!
Away from Mary with your warm bud breasts
An' your lips breathin' warm
I am cold.
   Mammy, how wise you are!
Can't you cover me?
Mammy, you grow cold too:
An' your skin is damp earth.
Nothin' that's warm can cover up my coldness.
Cold white world—I'll make you warm—that'll warm me!

—There's a white dream stands between my mouth and Mary's,
A white sunbeam in my soul.
I'll climb it. Tha's what it's fo'! I'll vault with the white sunbeam!

Empty pale world . . . world of the Free,
Wait till I come an' warm you: wait till I come an' fill you.

—Mary, the world is proud: world's a white far-away woman,
But she's waitin' fo' me to pour my flame inside her.
That ain't hate, Mary: she is waitin' fo' me!
    O Mammy, you're wise!
    O Mammy, how little wisdom helps when you're cold.

With a similar lyrical stream from Virginia Hade, in her bed,
the ominous grows large. She identifies night with Negroes:

—Yes, you are black:
Night, you're a raping nigger!
And the autumn day
        with its golden sun
        and its copperglow of leaf
        and its red earth
I suppose you think you're white?

—I am a white soul naked
        worn away and weary
Under the flood of color
Washed in the color sea
That is world, that is life!

—Lord, won't you let me sleep?
Look: I'm stretched out.
The poison can flow away, if only You'll let it.
Sleep without dream . . .
Tomorrow is work again.

—Sleep . . . dream world . . .
God, that's a Nigger too!
Color! Color! Color!
Everywhere.
Perhaps death is white? . . .

Her emotions flow back and forth, repulsed and attracted by
the idea of color. "I am all dark inside" she says; then, "Let

a nigger drown./ God breeds 'em." Finally she resolves her
thoughts:

> —My soul's not white!
>   Death's white: my soul wants to live.
>   It cries to live,
>   It sings to live,
>   It stirs within me like an unborn babe,
>   bleeding to live, all bloody with my blood . . .
>   And my white breast says No.
>
> —Why does the world say No?
>   Why don't I dare to learn how to say Yes?
>
> —Soul, you're a little black babe under my heart.
>   Yes you are . . . I say it . . .
>   Black as night
>   red as earth
>   golden as the sun
>   my soul. . . .

Within the two, as sleep overcomes them—indeed, the resolution that brings the sleep—is attraction to the other race,
personified with sexual feeling. "World's a far-away white
woman," he thinks; "—Soul, you're a little black babe under
my heart," she responds.

Dawn awakens both black and white Nazareth. The feeling
of enmity with the white race in John—recalled from injustices
of the past: "an iron grille shuts off a white farm whose pecans
and oranges and honey are not for niggers . . . an iron bridge
(niggers built it and twenty white men have their names on
the plate)" and of the day before: "—Dey let a nigger drown!
Dey smile an' say: Shall I wet my white trousers jes' 'cause a
nigger'd drown?"—these mingle with the present as he has to
be subservient to white men who make bad jokes, emphasizing
their position as masters. His path crosses that of Virginia Hade,

and he watches her, not realizing that her father is walking beside him. Judge Hade speaks:

"I have been walkin' by yo' side all of this street. An' yo' didn't see me."

He gives these words with a prophetic dryness. John feels the ominous threat of the knowing beneath them.

"*I've watched you, nigger,*" they say, "*I've watched you lookin' at my daughter. How dare you look at my daughter? Nigger, that look in yo' eyes means murder in our land. How dare you, nigger, look so hard at my daughter that you forget to salute the white man at yo' side?*"

"Beg pa'don, sah."

Judge Hade, in his office, senses the turbulence that is just beneath the surface, and cites John's action to Virginia, saying that he looked at her the way she, a moment before, was staring at the Negro girls outside picking oranges. " 'Father,' she said, 'you're the one that's sick . . . you and Bob and the whole lot of you men. . . . What are you men afraid of?' "

"Daughter, you're smart. Smart enough to run this business by yourself. That I allow. But you-all ain't smart enough to run the South."

Within their argument, emerging from it, is a lyrical passage that Beach, in *The Twentieth Century Novel*, appropriately calls a "dialogue between races." A passage of poetic prose, speaking for the whites, is replied to by a passage of verse, the voice of the Negro. The two races seem to be haunting each other, each feeling that the other is out of place; in the Negro song the whites fade into ghosts and then into distant memories:

> We goes rollin', we goes strong,
> We is a great big thunderin' song!
> Whar are you?
> Whar a r e yo'-all?

White town? Da's funny. I's heard tell o' dat
Dim, dim, dim, white town.
Why, sho! I's done heard tell o' dat.

The white song grows in hate:

—All the world's color: and I must hold my pride against the
world. Pride is white. History is white. The Christ is white.
Honor is white, and birthright. All else . . . color. The sky and
the sun and the stars, the trees and the thirsty soil: the eyes of
my beloved and her lips . . . color, color, foe to my high white-
ness. And you fight me, and you suck me dry. Even my heart is
color. In my mother's womb, I lay in blood: I was born, I was
conceived in dark hot hours. I must be white . . . and Christ is
very dim.

—*You-all don' count. Whah do you come in?*
Ah kin raise co'n 'n' taters
Ah kin hitch mah mule
Ah kin still co'n likker
Ah kin love mah girl.
You-all don' count. . . . Whah do you-all come in?

—Shouting, standing, rolling your hot eyes. Leave me be! Be earth!
Don't break into my slumber and my dreams!

On the impetus of that section's furious passion, flowing
equally from the dim white Chist and the hate, the third
section, "Noon," opens in the revival tent. The fire hose principle of making the outlet smaller to increase the force of the
stream is shown in action:

The Tent of Revival is a furnace. The fire in the sky has begun
to slide, slide down: but the smolder of Nazareth at meeting rises.
The Tent of Nazareth is a furnace with piddling outlets. *Thou
Shalt Not Steal, Thou Shalt Not Lust, Thou Shalt Not Play or
Dance* . . . what outlets these for the thick smoke of Nazareth?
The wooden preacher and his Christ kindle the mass of the
crowd. Passion snakes under laps, swirls up: passion murmurs

within narrow brows: there is a larval silence that is flame . . .
stifling, curling, spreading within the ice-hot shadows of the Tent,
and no way outward save these little holes, stopped long since by
the vague smut of usage.

Thou shalt not. . . . Thou shalt not. . . .

LET ME FLAME UP
LET ME FLAME OUT
LET THE WORLD BURN FOR ME!

Employing the same technique all writers of intense atmosphere use, building up an emotion, and holding it in abeyance
through a calming or relieving passage, then building again,
Frank in the twelfth chapter reports a calm conversation between John and Virginia; because of the heat and the revival,
a holiday is called. She goes to the revival tent, then turns away,
encountering her father and brother going to the meeting. She
tells them that she is going for a walk; she is going where it is
cool.

We then follow John's wanderings through Niggertown into
the woods, and to the edge of the bay. He strips off his clothes
and dives into the water, and as he cuts through the surface,
Virginia steps from the trees onto the shore. The chapters in
this part of the novel are like breakers in an incoming tide. Each
starts before the time the previous one ended, and each goes
farther. We go back to Virginia as she walked through Niggertown, pity and rage toward the Negroes mingling in her. Mary
Cartier watches her go the same direction that John had taken,
and we feel with her that the race barrier may be broken by
what will follow.

The scene of Virginia watching John swim, watching him
naked on the shore, is reminiscent of Whitman's woman watching the men swimming. She too participates in her mind—is
naked in her imagination. But then she sits under a tree and
awaits him, and they talk freely, the race barrier for the moment

broken. When it looms again, he brings out his knife and whittles on a twig. Her response is to lift her skirt and pull a pen-knife from her stocking. As he sees her do so, his knife slips and he cuts his thumb; the knife-blade reddens with his blood. She suggests they swap. He examines the two knives: his, large and clumsy, with a black wood handle and a thick notched blade; hers, tiny, mother-of-pearl, white veined with blue. " ' 'Tain't a fair bargain,' he judges slowly. 'Not for you, and not for me, it ain't fair.' " She insists, and their hands approach each other. She is stronger than he, in the spiritual struggle that ensues, but in bowing before that strength, in obeying her, he regains his power, seeing her ". . . Unreal face, all naked before his: it is like a forest in the high noon of summer stripped sudden of its leaves. . . . She sees him: unreal, too. In his eyes snow: his body is flame, but his eyes snow. . . ." He walks away.

By making their intercourse symbolic, Frank has not only insured against grotesquery, but has indicated a superiority in John. Leaving taste entirely out of it—for we have seen before that when it interferes with the artistic logic of his writing, Frank utterly ignores taste—John still must not have intercourse with Virginia. Sexual intercourse, in Frank's ethic, implies equality; it is not surrender of one to the other, but a sacred act engaged in by both. Like the mass, it can be sung backward and made a symbol of evil, but that would be as much out of place in *Holiday* as it would be for Virginia to wipe out race hatred in Nazareth. She is not evil enough to be raped nor good enough to wipe out the evil in the place. The outcome of the story, too, is resultant from their not having had intercourse, for if they had, Virginia would not have betrayed John. A sociological novelist might develop their affair and eventually show John being lynched and Virginia disgraced when the news, as it of course must, seeped out: but that, to freshen a cliché, would be another story; and its point would seem to be in opposition to Frank's.

Symbols become mixed, or operate on more levels, as the conclusion of the scene comes. Virginia cuts herself at the waist, of course symbolizing the knife as a sexual organ; but at the same time, her act is one of betrayal, since it is through being cut with John's knife, rather than through anything she says, that she has him lynched. Both symbols are presented as unconscious on Virginia's part.

Part Four, "Dusk," opens again in the revival tent. It is necessary to build up again the tension to revival meeting pitch. The crowd emerges from the tent with portions of the emotion clinging to them, turned partly into symbols and, since the meeting was not a satisfactory one, sex unconsummated, like an incomplete orgasm. The crowd chatters:

> . . . Voices thickly dryly twine a straw tangle through the slow mass moving up to Main Street; angular bodies bowing faint gesticulant sharp pent jets of easelessness at play up out from the horizontal pace to Main Street; maze of eye-seek, lip-curl, finger-twist-and-jerk within the sluggish forward of the way to Main Street; choked breast, clamped heart-leap, gnaw of the spark a cancer in their brains throb shuttle thresh deliberate slow to Main Street: HALT
>
> Virginia Hade

There is an ease, almost a calm in the way the crowd prepares for the lynching. Virginia keeps telling them, "I'm all right," until her father takes her home. The preacher makes a futile gesture (almost intentionally futile) at stopping them, and he calmly lets himself be unheard: "I have done my duty."

While benches are dragged from the revival tent into the square, and a tree is prepared, the mob sweeps into Niggertown, whose residents are out of sight. John, having refused to run away, is with Mary and his mother when they find him; and

the crowd is swayed for a moment by his dignity and the love
the women bear him. Bob Hade mockingly asks if he expects the
women to save him:

"You know better, yo'self, than to think I grouped 'em there."
His words, cold and flinchless, strike in a single blow against
the group of men.

They are man and youth and man. A subtle rotting threatens
the Rope, threatens the Iron Paling: threatens to make them
men with eyes to see this quiet straight man and his molten
women . . .

—She is lovely. That breast is in pain. I have
       lain in such a breast.
   Save me, Rope! Save me from that bitter longing.

—He looks honest. He looks clean. Perhaps it is
       I who am wrong.
   High steel spikes of my Pride
   Save me from being wrong!
   Save me from feeling low!

—What do we know? Whom have we asked? Ask him.
   What can a nigger answer
   When we ask for blood?

—She is a mother too. Mammy o' mine, you'd have
       such arms around me
   If they hunted me.
   Can I go back to you?
   No; I can blot you out.

—But she is lovely, young. It's she he loves.
       They love each other
           There might be a mistake.
   No mistake this: I can't touch your black breast!
   No mistake this: I can't touch your deep song!

—ROPE: SAVE ME ROPE
   SPIKE ME AROUND IN SAFETY, IRON FENCE

FENCE OF HATE SAVE ME
FENCE OF HATE SHUT OUT THAT FLOOD
CUP OF DEATH, COOL ME
COOL ME, STEEL. . . .

Virginia in her bed hears the murmur of the crowd waiting in the square, knowing she can stop it. "—Will I go? . . . And what is 'saving'? . . . And what is 'John Cloud'?" Hypnotized by the question "—Will I go?" she lies in her bed through the noise of the lynching, and when silence comes, she sleeps. And "The *Psyche* stands at the empty pier that points from Nazareth out into the world."

9

Chalk Face

ON PAGES 33-5 OF NOTEBOOK VIII IS A "THEME FOR MYSTERY story." Now this is astonishing, for Waldo Frank is congenitally incapable of following stylized conventions, and no form is more conventional, or has less to do with values, than the mystery story. Since its origin in the three tales of "ratiocination" of Edgar Poe, it has not changed, nor has any significant device been added to it. By June 18, two months and five days from the completion of *Holiday*, the mystery story, tentatively called "Who is a Man," was in rough draft. The rest of 1923, until Frank departed for Europe in October, was well-filled with work. He translated Jules Romains' novel *Lucienne*, gave a series of lectures on "The Revolution in Art and Literature" at the Rand School, and worked on a number of essays. The last month before sailing Frank added to all the others the job of preparing his collection of essays, *Salvos*, for the press.

In Paris this vitality was shifted in another direction. *Our America*, *City Block*, and *Rahab* had made him famous. He was lionized by the French, and an epigram, *Pour la Nouvelle Revue Française, la littérature américaine, c'est Waldo Frank*, was circulated. He was received with honor at Shakespeare and Company, and he and James Joyce exchanged inscribed copies of *Ulysses* and *City Block*. He noted when he returned to his notebook in Madrid, in February, 1924: "Nov.-Dec. Dismal lionizing & painful gaiety in Paris. NO WORK." In moving from Paris to Madrid, he went by way of Marseilles, Algiers, Bou-Saada, Morocco, and Seville. Obviously, first in his mind was his book on Spain, and it was only incidentally, while steeping himself in Moorish life during a month in Bou-Saada, that he corrected and typed his novel, now entitled *To Life*.

While Frank continued gathering impressions for his book on Spain, he sent the novel back to the United States. On March 21, his publisher, Horace Liveright, sent him this cable: UNANIMOUSLY FEEL SHOULD NOT PUBLISH TO LIFE WHICH FIVE OF US HAVE READ STOP WOULD NOT SELL AND WOULD HURT YOU. On May 27, Liveright followed up this and another cable with a letter explaining that when he first cabled he had not read the novel. By April 18, when he cabled the second time, he had, and then had urged that the book be rewritten to make it clearer to the average reader. He excused his first cable on the grounds of the poor sale of *Salvos*, and indicated confidence in the novel. The main purpose of the letter seems to have been to persuade Frank to agree to doing some revising and to accepting the title *Chalk Face*. He enclosed a copy of the picture for the dust jacket, showing that he was anxious to get the book and willing to spend money on having a jacket designed in the hope that the title and conditions would be agreed to. Horace Liveright saw virtues in the novel, and although he realized that not everyone would see them, since at least five of his associates did not, he felt that the obscurity could be cleared up by revision. Frank, however, had gone on to other interests, chiefly the book on Spain, and although the Bou-Saada manuscript differs a trifle from the printed copy, the book submitted from Spain is, in the main, the book that was published.

Nevertheless, *Chalk Face* does not seem to be a difficult story to understand. Certainly anyone who can appreciate Poe's "William Wilson" will be able to follow it with ease, for not only would he have the capacity to understand *Chalk Face*, but he would also have a knowledge of Poe's story as a guide. It is true, as Liveright pointed out in his letter of May 27, 1924, that the dedicatory epistle offers the book to Frank's father because they both have a weakness for mystery stories; but it goes on to clarify rather than make confusion for one who might mistake the book, on that account, for a standard whodunit.

The similarity of *Chalk Face* to the fiction of Edgar Poe is noticeable from the first page; the very sentence rhythms are like Poe's. John Mark is a Poe-like character, brooding, introverted, an idealizer of a woman, an engager in a mysterious intellectual activity which involves the mixture of ancient learning and modern science. His attitude toward Mildred is the same as that of a Poe character toward his beloved, needing a woman as an ingredient in his life, and choosing her because she is the most perfect of women—just as he might select a Rolls Royce when he felt the need of a car. She, however, is quite different from Poe's dying women; she is stronger, in every respect, and healthier, than John Mark. Deeper than these details, however, there is the same sort of dream logic as can be found in Poe's work. John Mark, in the person of the white-faced man, murdered Philip LaMotte before he heard of him! *Chalk Face* is a work which delves into the same recesses of the unconscious, where insanity lurks, as the stories of Poe.

A simple explanation for the similarity would be that Frank consciously was imitating Poe. This seems not to be so. As he remembers it today, he noticed the similarity first after the book was written. Even discounting his memory, thirty years later, of not having been thinking of Poe or reading Poe, there is evidence that he was not, and no evidence that Poe was in any way on his mind. In March, 1923, just before the idea for the story came to him, he listed the books he felt had had the greatest influence on him: The Bible, Aeschylus, Racine, Balzac, Spinoza, Villon, Whitman, Romains. Poe is mentioned twice in *Salvos*; each time in a list of American authors. It was not until December 30, 1925, after the publication of *Chalk Face* that, in a review of the Valentine letters, Frank wrote anything about Poe, and that article was written after the first of December. Indeed, there is no evidence that Frank to this day considers Poe's fiction great art. He says in *The Re-Discovery of America*, "I consider him a mediocre poet, a writer of poor prose, an artist wholly unachieved." With that attitude, he would hardly choose Poe as a model, although he could subconsciously use his methods; however it is highly unlikely that in 1924 he would associate Poe's objectives with his, and there is no reason to think that he did.

Disregarding the literary merit of *Chalk Face* in relation to the work of Edgar Poe, we can find in the novel a deviation from the rapid growth of Waldo Frank as a writer of fiction. The two phases of the development of the lyrical novel came with great rapidity after the mystical experience early in 1920. From the stories conceived before the war and the techniques developed in his first two published novels he created *City Block*. Through experimenting in *Rahab* with a combination of the *City Block* lyrical strain and the larger scale of *The Dark Mother* he achieved the lyrical continuity of *Holiday*. They are equal in their spiritual profundity, but different in method; the change was necessary unless Frank was to continue writing *City Blocks* for the rest of his career. But *Chalk Face* twists inward.

The entry referred to in Notebook VIII, 33-5, reads as follows:

John Mark spends the evening with his lady love, and while he is there, his rival is murdered in his chambers, two miles away. John feels, strangely, a sense of implication, almost of guilt which he cannot understand. So he constitutes himself sleuth. The police find the solution easy. Brain was alone: the bell rang: he let in two men who claimed to have a message and killed him. Scared: hence no robbery. But John finds in a corner an envelope addressed "Philip Brain" in the hand of Gladys . . . empty. Was there a note in it? Gladys claims she never had that sort of envelope, nor wrote with that sort of green ink. Envelope & ink are like John's.

John has a dream that weirdly haunts him: (presented not as a dream but as narrative) He is in a house on top of a hill: there are two rooms, separated by a long corridor. The other room is dark. In this room, lighted cozily with many shadows by a lamp, are John, Brain, Gladys, Gladys' parents, etc. A strange light comes up the hill: a ghost! They watch & behold within it a sort of mass of gray undulating flesh. Gradually, as it mounts the hill-slope, it takes on the shape of a man. It disappears from the window-range: they all know it is in the other room! John resolves to explore. He goes down the dark corridor into the other room, and there is a handsome boy ghost. John finds him splendid [?] & is not afraid of him & talks to him. Then he touches him & he is real! He is scared & goes down the corridor to the room & opens the door: & there are all the company again, *but they have become ghosts. Only the ghost boy & he are real.* "Am I a ghost?"

John wakes in a horror of sweat. Is this the key to the drama? Is he part ghost and man— & as a ghost did he kill his rival, Brain? His father & mother, motoring, have inexplicable accident and he is their heir? Did he have aught to do with this also? Gladys adores him: he is rich: yet he [word unreadable] in despair. Can he go to Police & say: arrest my ghost—a murderer!

Denouement: when he meets the ghost in a ghastly night. and the ghost wins. He dies.

Waldo Frank recalls that he made this entry in his notebook after being awakened by a dream, which suggested it. His dream was, it appears, the dream narrative of the note, set in the house on the top of the hill; the preliminary matter of the murder and the envelope was probably an associated exposition—the background of memory of the actor in the dream. The fragmentary construction of the sentences in the last paragraph of the note is matched by increasing haste in the handwriting; very likely the disciplined subconsious of the writer was taking over from the recollections of the dream.

In the finished novel, John Mark becomes John Mark, M.D., a brilliant scientist who has studied in all the famous foreign schools and has accepted an ill-paying job at the Institute to pursue his research. He has a small income, but his parents are wealthy. His love is Mildred, daughter of a very wealthy man, whom he loves because he finds in her the spiritual chastity that he has sought in vain in other women; an odd sort of chastity, since he found in prostitutes "a low chastity [that] is at times the one quality they possess." But he wants to be able to support Mildred in the fashion to which she is accustomed without interrupting his research at the Institute. He asks his parents for financial help, and they refuse: "If you marry, like every other married man, you got to look out for yourself," his father tells him.

The personality of John Mark, not expressed in the note although it may have been in Frank's mind when he wrote it, is justification of much of the action. He is arrogant and thoroughly assured of his superiority. A good rule in Waldo Frank's writing is, where you see the name Mark, there is Waldo Frank. David Markand, John Mark, Mark Ferry, all these are facets of Waldo Frank. John Mark is a projection of Waldo Frank at the peak of his fame looking on to greater things he will do if the details of living would only get out of the way. Of course, the character in the novel goes far beyond any self-assurance in Frank; John Mark goes right up to the brink of insanity and looks over the edge. "The gross man is nourished with gross food," he says, "the indifferent man with any food at all. My high work called for high fuel. Not for a drudge, not for a harried woman, nor a pretty one, nor for promiscuous pleasures. For Mildred! The essential Mildred! Nothing less."

It would be possible to go to ridiculous lengths in "proving" Chalk Face a sublimation of Frank's own feelings. His parents and his wife's were well-to-do. As an artist, making contributions to the culture of the country, he looked with envy on those who were better rewarded than he while they made little or no cultural contribution; yet he would not abandon his calling for anything. In addition, his wife had an active career and was making contributions to the nation's culture in her own right, and he had a rival for her love in his son. Obviously it would be ridiculous to attribute to him a wish to murder his son and his parents so he could be properly nourished in his art —but the circumstances of his life at the time indicate an analogous feeling of unconscious resentment for these people, one which is psychologically present in all fathers and children; and it is by the projection of these, his own experiences and impulses, that the artist is able to create. None of this application of Frank's own possible feelings is evident in the note recorded at the time the idea for the story first hit him; from its place at the end and the way the handwriting indicates increasing haste in putting it down, it is evident that the part of the parents in the story was an afterthought. The scene in which John is refused money by his parents was inserted at Bou-Saada. Changing Gladys to Mildred would suggest a later identification of the heroine with Frank's wife, whose name, Margaret, is not likely to suggest the name Gladys. The changing of Philip Brain to Philip LaMotte—from a brain to a lump—suggests an infant; although here things begin to be stretched too thin.

Without making too much of what the name changes suggest, it is possible to see that they typify one kind of change that was made in the conception of the story; the materials were moved into Frank's experience and then projected from it, through the use of his knowledge of abnormal psychology. Another kind of change transformed the doppelgänger twist from the Poe-like symbol of the inseparability of evil from the human character; in the book the ghost loses, dies, and John Mark, freed of evil, survives. From the moment he became aware of it, John Mark pursued his other self, and as his awareness of it grew, he gradually gained power over it. Unlike the note, when

the two murders take place in the book, John is made aware of
them. During the first, he is walking toward Mildred's house,
thinking of the dilemma of needing both his work and Mildred.
As he thinks deeply of her, he sees her as a means to a higher
life, and suddenly he finds himself seeing with an omniscient
eye:

> I can fly where I will, and enter where I want. I see myriad
> women's arms, suddenly free and fragile like their hair. Women's
> arms wave, like hair, in a great wind. A wind sweeps my maze of
> images: I see streaming men and women and children. Each is
> crouched close to another. They do not see how they are streaming.
> They think of themselves as fixed, all else as moving.
>
> But I am moving. Something in me is fixed, and something in
> me is moving! . . .
>
> . . . .
> This is a pleasant room, and I am in it.

The room he sees himself in is a luxurious private library,
with a dark man in it, who looks "like one of the saints on the
great Porch at Chartres." John sees him die; sees a knife in his
breast—and the vision is over.

When he arrives at Mildred's, he learns that he has a rival,
like him in that she would grant either a kiss, or would agree to
go off with either for a week. Instead, each asks that she marry
him, and she is not sure enough of her affections to take so
permanent a step. This is his first knowledge of the existence of
his rival, and until the telephone rings and Mildred learns of
the murder, John knows only his first name. Moreover, although
motive for the murder that has already been committed exists
from the moment John learns of Philip's existence, it is not
until the next day that the provocation comes to his knowledge,
when by means of a cryptic note on LaMotte's engagement pad,
John learns that Mildred was about to have an assignation with
him.

His consciousness of the second murder is more elusive. To

present it, Frank invented two more characters: the wise scientist Dr. Isaac Stein, and a medium who John's colleagues assure him is authentic. After visiting Philip LaMotte's rooms and seeing the body (as a member of the Institute he has a police card), John works on the problem of the murder by sitting, like Sherlock Holmes or Dupin, in his room for two weeks thinking. Then he feels the urge to walk, and following a meandering course, one that keeps turning back to Sixth Avenue, he comes eventually to the Sixth Avenue room of Mrs. Landsdowne, the medium. She tells him how he has come, and says, "You are the sort who knows . . . why have you come here?" When he asks her what he has done, she replies instead, "What are you doing now?" On returning to his room he meets Dr. Stein, and after they talk for a while and the doctor is about to leave, John notices the same look in his eyes that he had noticed in Mrs. Landsdowne's. John asks what it is he has seen. ". . . your will, John Mark—" Dr. Stein replies, "what is it touching?" We learn what it was touching when, a few moments later, the telephone rings and John learns that his parents have been in an automobile accident.

In the dream episode the style changes from a Poe-esque introspection to a simple reporting in uncomplicated sentences, most of them with one subject and one predicate, and many of them short. But the figures and actions are all symbolic, and the simplification of language plus the use of what are clearly symbols creates a dreamlike atmosphere of unreality. Among the people are John's dead parents and Philip LaMotte, as well as Mildred, her father, Dr. Stein, and John. Mildred's father plays solitaire; John's parents are chatting with Dr. Stein, his father enjoying his cigar as he did when they were talking money early in the book. Philip and John stand close together, watching Mildred as she sings old English ballads to a guitar. As in the vision early in the book, she is dressed in green. Between songs, they talk of how high the house is perched on its hilltop, and speculate on the dawn that they will see sooner than will other people and that will shoot up from below. Although it is midnight, Mildred wonders if they will be able to see the dawn soon, and John goes to the window to watch for it. He sees a light moving up the hill, and at that point the others in the room begin to fade. They do not hear him tell what he sees until he has spoken for the third time; then they cluster around the window and watch the light form into a youth. When the ghost goes into the other room, the actions of all the people become overt symbols: John's mother locks the door; his father says, " 'I have heard no one say what we have seen. We have seen nothing.' 'Let's get back,' says Mr. Fayn, 'To our game.' 'These phenomena,' warns Doctor Stein, 'are beyond our grasp. . . .' " Philip turns to Mildred; she turns to John. John goes into the corridor. The experience with the ghost, in which John and the ghost change places, remains unchanged, but when John returns, the others do not see him, and although he can see them he cannot touch them. His hands go through them as through a light. He screams and awakens.

His awakening is into an experience that is as much dream as the other, save that he retains an evidence of its reality. Urged by the puzzle of the dream, he leaves his house before dawn, and awaiting him is the youth of his dream, now ominous. All through the novel this other self is referred to as a man with a white head. The messenger admitted to Philip's apartment, obviously the murderer, appeared to the Negro porter to have a colorless head, even his eyes being white. The police considered that vision the imagining of a superstitious simpleton. The mysterious man who applied for work at the garage where John's parents' car was kept, and who could have loosened the lug-nuts when he was left alone for a moment, according to the mechanic, had a white head. This white headed man goads John now to the river, onto a ferry, and to the edge of a quarry. But the ghost is killed, not, as in the note, John.

For three weeks John considers his next act; then he makes an appointment with Mildred and confesses to her. She first thinks he is mad; then she realizes that his madness is a more complex thing. Here the printed text differs markedly from the Bou-Sa-ada Ms. This scene was originally related by John in a postscript; in the book it is narrated dramatically, making clear that John asked her for salvation. He tells her that he has been ruthless in his pursuit of her as an aid to his life, dedicated to the seek-ing of truth; but that now he realizes that what he was seeking can only be achieved by mutual devotion in love. She, however, refuses, leaving him to seek salvation without her help.

Thus the postscript, by being moved entirely out of the ex-periences of John Mark and back into the experiences of Waldo Frank, forms a link between the dream world and actuality. In the name of John Mark, Frank tells us of watching the harmoni-ous and peaceful scene of an evening alone in the Berkshire Hills. He watches the birds—then sees the tooth and claw in the scene: an owl terrifying a thrasher; robins devouring worms; a woodpecker massacring woodslugs. "No single creature in that gentle dusk, but was engaged in bitter desperate war. And I sat, idle, burning my tobacco, slaying the mosquito that dared to buzz within the reach of my majesty." He concludes:

> Out of the ash that you call history, rises the eternal flame of Love. Warm yourselves there, my brothers and my sisters. For the time will come when you will watch Love's distant gleam, desperate and nostalgic like a winter moth which beats on the frosted win-dow trying to get in where the light burns, which beats and beats until it falls emaciate in the snow. . . .

The illness and recovery of *Chalk Face* represents a difficult transition in the life of Waldo Frank, when he was faced with crises in his personal and his artistic life; when he needed to face the split that all public figures suffer when their acclaim steals privacy from them; and when he was attracted by a different kind of activity in the form of his cultural study of Spain. Although *Virgin Spain* is, I am told by Spanish authorities, the finest study of that country of recent times (one says that as an interpretation of their country to the Spanish, it is on a par with *Don Quixote*), Frank realized even then that it was only a part of a larger plan. His objective as always was America. Even before the Great War, he had visualized America as one, a potential cultural entity that would embrace all that is good in America, North and South. To understand America Hispana he needed first to go to the source, Spain; and to understand Spain he needed to seek out its roots in Africa. This was a large project. He knew that it would keep him from fiction for a time; he did not realize how long.

Frank today says that he abandoned the lyrical novel after *Chalk Face* because the vein had run out. That would seem to be at least partly a modest oversimplification; considering all else he did the year after the last lyrical novel was sent to the publisher, it is no wonder that he did not turn out another immediately. From March, 1924, to June, 1925, he wrote sixty-nine articles—among them some of the first *New Yorker* profiles—*Virgin Spain*, and two plays. During the rest of 1925 he wrote twenty-eight more articles and two short stories. Certainly Frank had all the fluency he had had before, and *Virgin Spain*, one can easily see, required as much creative energy as any novel could. Clearly there was a great drive in him toward cultural studies rather than fiction. Horace Liveright kept urging him to turn back to fiction, even up to 1928, when, in acknowledging that Scribner's would publish *The Re-Discovery of America*, he asked again for the novel that he had been promised since 1926.

Eric Ely-Estorick, in an otherwise quite muddled article on Waldo Frank, makes a useful pair of statements: "In the division of Mr. Frank's writings which he calls Story, the subject is a person or group of persons. In History, the subject is a people." The development of Waldo Frank the person was directly expressed in the lyrical novels; indeed, I suspect that he developed through writing the lyrical novels—that they were laboratory experiments through which he discovered himself. Having developed the concept of the Person, aware of himself in relation to the Whole and the Whole in himself, he felt driven to apply that development on the level of society. First the person, then the people. He rose to the level of *City Block* and *Holiday*; then pursued the course that led him through *Virgin Spain* to *America Hispana, The Re-Discovery of America*, and *Dawn in Russia*. A similar pattern is observable in two more steps; the symphonic novels, *The Death and Birth of David Markand* and *The Bridegroom Cometh* led to *Chart for Rough Waters, South American Journey*, and *The Jew in Our Day*; and the development which led up to his new lyrics, culminating up to now in *Not Heaven*, is soon to be expressed in Waldo Frank's as yet unpublished *Rediscovery of Man*. A more fundamental development, which could not have been visible when Estorick wrote his article, is that throughout this progress, Story and History are coming closer together. Waldo Frank's biography of Simon Bolívar, *Birth of a World*, is a study, at one time, of a person and a people. In the symphonic novels, Frank began bringing society into his fiction, with the objective of expressing a concept of the person in perspective of both the cosmos and society.

10

Cultures and Communism

FOR MANY YEARS FRANK WAS TO PLAN TO RETURN TO THE NOVEL —not this year, but next. In Notebook IX he planned for 1925-6 the completion of three plays, *Virgin Spain*, a volume of his *New Yorker* pieces, miscellaneous stories and essays, and even some lectures, so he would be able to devote the entire following year to the novel. Two of the plays were completed before the year was up, and some months later so was the third. All the miscellaneous pieces were written, and the *New Yorker* book, entitled *Time Exposures by Search-Light*, was prepared and published in October, 1926. The major work of the year, however, was *Virgin Spain*.

In *Virgin Spain* Frank continued the method of organization he had worked out for *Our America*—a comment on the roots of the country; impressionistic glimpses of various regions; examination of certain cultural phenomena such as the work of writers, artists, and musicians; and a prophetic conclusion. Modified to express the spirit of Spain, this method gained in intensity that makes *Virgin Spain* as great an expression of the creative imagination as any of Frank's novels—some would say greater.

After tracing the roots of Spain in Africa, both among the Moslems and the Jews, Frank turns to the region most recently recovered from the Moors, Andalusia; then, by way of contrast, to Aragon and Castile, following the route of the Cid and those

117

who drove back the Moors. Concluding his glimpses of the regions where certain of the ingredients of the Spanish spirit are found in varying degrees of emphasis, he discusses Valencia, leaving Catalonia and the land of the Basques for the prophetic third part, since they mark roads that the rest of Spain had not taken. The details for each region are drawn from history and architecture, significant customs, items of dress, and from literature. Descriptions and interpretations of the dances of the sections provide a common theme, linking and contrasting the ingredients of the culture.

The transition is not so abrupt as in Our America, therefore, to Part Two, where facets of the culture of the country as a whole are presented. The national is made to grow out of the regional as Frank traces the history of the will of the Kings of Spain, from Ferdinand to Isabella, to unify their country. Examples of the national tendency to irony and a sense of honor, remnants of the Moslem-Christian split and the power that welded them together, are shown in sections on the mystics of Spain, particularly St. John of the Cross and St. Theresa of Jesus. The channeling of the mystic tradition into action is traced through St. Ignatius Loyola and the jurist Francisco de Vitoria, its transformation into art in the development of the picaresque tale and a comparison of El Greco and Velázquez.

At the heart of the book are its two most remarkable chapters —one on Don Quixote and the other on the bullfight. In addition to its penetration as literary criticism, Frank's comments on Cervantes' work show it as a symbol of the Spanish mystic-realistic acceptance of two contradictory views—that of facts, and that of truth—assigning each to its place and accepting the validity of each. Irony and a sense of honor are the vital forces within the book of Cervantes; Frank finds the Don a symbol of Spain, medieval and modern but never undergoing the Renaissance. He says:

One and all, [the Prophets] encountered *reasons* which put their *truth* to flight. And the world was able to live whole within their truth only in ages which wilfully made reason servile. In the violence of his divorce from the world which he aspired to unite, in the ridiculousness of his discord from it, Don Quixote stands the last prophet of our historic Order. He bespeaks our need: a dynamic understanding which shall enlist ideal and reason, thought and act, knowledge and experience; which shall preserve the personal within the mystical will; which shall unite the world of fact in which we suffer all together with the world of dream in which we are alone. . . .

Ernest Hemingway devotes a long passage in his *Death in the Afternoon* to disparaging Frank's interpretation of the bullfight in *Virgin Spain*. Hemingway sees the *corrida* as a sportsman; his is the understanding of the participant, as the performing musician hears music, the artist studies the brush-strokes of a painting, or the craftsman looks at a piece of machinery. Frank studiously keeps himself remote, analyzing, interpreting, never becoming hypnotized or even excited. He finds the bullfight a drama—or ballet—conducted in a Roman circus. The first act, the provocation of the bull and the goring of a picador's horse (now forbidden in Spain) Frank finds a farce, in which the sacrificed nag is the comedian, the "patsy." The scene of the bandilleros, whom Frank finds "the critics, the epigrammatists, the *graciosos*, the chorus of the accelerant play" is a cleansing for the tragedy. The dance of the matador, a dance of death, becomes a symbol of the sexual act, Frank claims, even finding Christian symbolism in the Verónica. "The ancient orgy of Dionysus and Priapus is tinged with Christian pity." He concludes:

Gross comedy of blood; sex, dionysian and sadistic; the ancient rites of the brute and of the Christ meet here in the final image of stability. Spain's warring elements reach their locked fusion—

Spain's ultimate form. For although everything is in the bull ring, and although anything may happen, *nothing happens*. Circus, blood, dance, death equate to nullity. Like life in Spain, this spectacle is self-sufficient, issueless. . . .

The contrast resultant from following this intense symbol of Spain with the two regions of exceptional heritage, where the regional and the Spanish are at odds enables Frank to move into a discussion of the recent writers of Spain, also part Spanish part European. He then concludes with a prophetic conversation between Cervantes and Columbus, looking toward the new world and envisioning the birth of a new Spain there, after the dominance of the United States has come to an end.

Virgin Spain was soon translated into Spanish, and it is in Spain and Latin America that it has been most deeply appreciated. Although Frank favored the Loyalist government during the Civil War, and wrote an additional chapter for *Virgin Spain* on the war, so great was the prestige of the book that the Franco regime did not suppress any but the added chapter, and the book is still in print and being sold in Spain.

Immediately after sending *Time Exposures* to the printer, about the time he was reading proof on *Virgin Spain*, Frank wrote in his notebook, "The urgency is now the novel—a clear whole year for that—*April 1926—April 1927*." Then, below, "*Revision: April 1, 1926*—Move toward novel, but do not dream of touching it." In May he visited the Isle of Pines with Hart Crane, and the entries in his notebook show an increasing interest in philosophical speculation. By August the novel had a title: David Markand: An American History; and planned for immediately after its completion was a book on the problem of value in the modern world. Value is what Frank was thinking about, his notebook shows. In his determination that the next job was to be the novel, he probably did not notice the significance of the satisfied tenor of the conclusion of his notebook musings: "*Real Progress* in my meditation on a religious method in modern life."

In January, 1927, he went to Europe, travelling to Poland, Palestine, and Egypt, finally arriving at St. Georges d'Oléron, in the Bay of Biscay, where he planned to stay all summer and write his novel. Although he wrote about fifty thousand words, later all abandoned, on the novel, his notebook contains only notes on mysticism and religion. When, in September, he returned to the United States, he began writing the book that, if the notebooks are any indication, he had really been wanting to write all the while that he had been struggling with the novel.

Frank wrote *The Re-Discovery of America* through most of 1928, the chapters being published in the *New Republic* almost as soon as they were written, being attached to a sort of "Our America—Second Series" that Herbert Croly had requested for the magazine, but quickly growing beyond the scope of mere social criticism. At the same time that Croly had ordered the series, the *Saturday Evening Post* had asked for a similar set of articles, to be paid for at their very superior rates, but Frank refused, apparently feeling that what would come out of the ideas and inclinations he was pursuing could not be made part of the *Post*.

When *Our America* appeared, it struck a need and an aspiration in the American people at just the right moment. *The Re-Discovery of America* penetrates more deeply in describing the American scene, and goes much farther in providing a pattern for the future, but it came at the wrong moment. The book fell into the vacuum between two eras. One of these eras was that which nurtured the esthetic revival of the twenties; the other created the political revival of the thirties. It was the same impulse, reacting in different people in different ways, that produced both the essentially hopeful and mystical writing of Frank, Anderson, Bourne, Brooks, Robinson, Frost, O'Neill, and even the early Hemingway, and produced the cynicism and despair of Scott Fitzgerald, T. S. Eliot, and E. E. Cummings. They described the same scene, and they did not disagree on what they saw, but only on what it meant. Toward the end of the twenties, the writings of all these people suffered a change. The time between Frank's last lyric novel and his first symphonic, the nine years between 1925 and 1934, corresponded exactly to the time between the first period of Fitzgerald's writing, ending with *The Great Gatsby*, and *Tender is the Night*. The novels that began appearing in the late twenties were novels of social protest, that expressed the need for political action. Dos Passos and Hemingway took this change in their stride, and a multitude of younger writers, among them James T. Farrell, came in with the new tide. *The Re-Discovery of America* is neither of the old nor of the new, although it contains elements of each, but it is an expository treatment of the ideas of the Person and the Whole, that Frank had worked out in his lyric novels, and contains an attempt to apply these ideas to the person of modern American society—at a time when the American was marching with like-minded fellows, to the stockbroker, to the bootlegger, to a demonstration for Sacco and Vanzetti, it did not matter which, Frank asked him to go off alone and meditate. An archetypical reaction was that of the English reviewer whose chief comment was that it was bad enough that America was discovered once: he wanted no truck with a rediscovery.

If its public had been receptive, there could have been no more important book for 1929 than *The Re-Discovery of America*. In post mortems of our flirtation with materialism, both the dialectical and the stocks and bonds varieties, Frank's ideas turn up in very strange company. Even today, to read it properly one must begin one's thinking, not in the context of recent history, but with the formation of modern society in ages past; it is a thorough reassessment of human behavior, an abandonment of the ego and its replacement with the mystic sense, organically one in Person and in People.

Frank begins by tracing the intellectual history of modern civilization through its basic convictions—the supremacy of man (under God), the power of reason and the senses as perceptors of reality, the absolutism of cause and effect, the independence of space and time from the human mind, and the individuality of human beings. Science, he finds, has dissipated the validity of each of these concepts. When a man could rely on all such order in the universe, he lived in harmony with the cosmos as he saw it: Dante's *Divine Comedy* expresses this harmony. But since Dante, there has been only discord. For a new harmony, Frank proposes the development of a sense of the Whole, founded on scientific fact, and operative not through any single sense but through the body as a unit.

In his descriptive passages on phenomena of modern life, the state of man as the hunted in the modern jungle, the gods and cults of power, the fetish of comfort, the delusions of press and art, the leaders, censors, women, and folk, Frank is acute and witty. Here is the material of *Our America* intensified. His observations are so penetrating and clever that multitudes of imitations of this part of the book have been successfully promoted.

Instead of presenting merely a report on the state of the nation, however, Frank goes on to offer a method for treating whatever ails us. He proposes that Americans become Persons, conscious of the Whole. He claims that a community of Persons —true Persons—would mean a community of truths. A method of meditation to bring about a consciousness of the Whole is his specific proposal. He does not provide a complete set of instructions on the procedure of becoming a Person; the section in which he discusses the matter is called merely "Notes on Method." It concludes, "Sparce suggestions, these notes, of what . . . developed . . . must be the subject of a book."

The method was not wholly worked out, for it evolved from the lyric novels and was a working toward the unity Frank was later to project between the Person and the People. In the notebooks he kept telling himself that he was staying away from the novel in part to turn out paying journalism; he planned to write for money only until he could take off enough time to complete the novel. When he took his year, he worked diligently on the novel, but was not satisfied with what he had done and abandoned it. Then when given the opportunity to turn out a routine job for the *Saturday Evening Post* and make great heaps of money, or to express on the social level a religious method he had found for himself, a long, hard job that would bring very little money, he chose the latter. He almost failed to get a hearing even through the *New Republic*, for none of the editors but Croly approved of the mystic tone of the later installments; yet in spite of opposition, he kept at it. This is clearly a choice situation. If he had really been ready to write the novel, he would have taken the *Saturday Evening Post* offer and bought himself the leisure; he did not, for he needed to express the method he had found whereby every man could become a Person.

Nineteen-twenty-nine and 1930 carried him in another direction, still not obviously that of the novel. The success of the Spanish translation of *Virgin Spain* brought an invitation to lecture in Mexico. This enabled him to put the cards down and make a definite decision about the novel: he had a new conception of its scope, which was to be greater than he had first planned; and he felt that the summons from Mexico was a "true call." He was by then fluent in Spanish; he could, therefore, communicate with Spanish-speaking Americans, seeming less like a visitor from abroad and more like a fellow-American. He went to Mexico, and from there to South America. His Spanish-American lectures were collected and published in Madrid for the whole Spanish-speaking world under the title *Primer Mensaje á la América Hispana*. It is not within the scope of this study to tell the fascinating and heartening story of Waldo Frank and America Hispana. An inkling of the mutual respect and affection existing between him and the Latin Americans can be gained, not only from his own books, but also from *Waldo Frank in America Hispana*, a collection of responses to Frank's tour, edited by M. J. Benardete.

In *America Hispana*, the book completed the year after Frank's return from his tour of South America, he attempts to trace the cultural history of that continent according to the method of *Virgin Spain*. Because of its greater complexity, the portrait of South America is a fabric with more threads to it, a pattern, since not yet worked out, more difficult to describe. Frank nevertheless works from the terrain through the culture of the Indian civilizations to the influence of Spain. He treats five areas: the Andes, the Pampa, the Pacific, the Amazon forest, and the Caribbean area.

Of most importance is his vision of the America to be, an integration of the two Americas into a spiritually whole people of the future. Leading to this through sketches of the careers of San Martín and Bolívar, he draws on his impressions as presented in *Virgin Spain* and *The Re-Discovery of America* to show the potentialities for a society conscious of the Whole. His unit of operation is, as always, the Person.

Throughout his writings, Frank up to this point had disparaged the efficacy of practical political action. Nevertheless, politics was a force that can be seen increasingly pulling at him. Social consciousness he had from his father, and as in most things, he went beyond his father in that too. The revolutionary movement was interesting to all the writers of the *Seven Arts*, and Frank early associated revolution in society with revolution in the soul, expressing his feeling in a prose poem, "Holy Russia," printed in that magazine in 1917. In the years of reaction that followed the war he poked fun at the Babbitts in his *New Yorker* pieces while he wrote seriously on higher cultural problems. But with the crash on Wall Street and the ensuing poverty and want in the United States, he was driven by conscience to take a more active part in the urgency of social injustice. This was largely theoretical up to the time that he became chairman of a committee of American writers formed to send food to the striking miners in Harlan and Bell Counties in Kentucky. With others, Frank was escorted to the state line and beaten by pro-operator vigilantes. For the first time the bandage-swathed head of Waldo Frank appeared in the popular press.

The ensuing publicity and the image of Frank as one "wounded on the barricades," made him a hero to the political left, and although he certainly could never be a follower of anybody's line, much less that of the Communist Party, he worked with the Communists because he felt they were the most active fighters for social justice. He had visited Russia in 1931, and his *Dawn in Russia* appeared a few months after the Kentucky incident, so that the book, which was sharply critical of much he found in Russia, was not disapproved by the critics of the left.

Dawn in Russia is written with a lighter touch than almost any other work of Frank's. It is probably his only book that could properly be considered a travel book, really little more than an account of his travels. Although the last section, "Meditation on the Atlantic," does a bit of conclusion drawing, and ties together the significant details of the earlier parts that show some of the peculiar reaction produced by the admixture of Marx's scientific rationalist materialism on the complex of peoples and beliefs of traditional Russia, the book is attractive today —almost charming in a whimsical way—as a record of the juxtaposition of anti-authoritarian, anti-materialist but comfort-loving Waldo Frank and the authoritarian and bureaucratic "New Communist Man." When he wanted anything, from news of when a boat or train would leave to permission to enter a closed zone, he went to the GPU! From the time he arrived

in Leningrad, leaving his guide to carry his bags to the hotel
while he took a walk on the Nevsky Prospekt mixing with the
crowd, until on his last day in Moscow he stood in line to visit
Lenin's tomb, he obeyed impulse and ignored itineraries in a
way impossible today. His interpreter left behind protesting, he
plunged into the slums seeking Dostoevsky's old room; taken
to a court session he dragged his guide to the adjoining court-
rooms; and he was able to laugh at himself, a representative of
the bourgeoisie, haggling with the remaining capitalists then
left in Russia, the droschke drivers, both resenting their high
prices and sympathizing with them since they always had to buy
on the free market. Throughout, he was sympathetic but critical.

After the appearance of *Dawn in Russia*, following so close
on the Kentucky incident, Frank came very close to being
spokesman for the writers of the political left. He spoke and
wrote for and helped to form the League of American Writers;
his books were published in Russia with great success, and he was
one of the few writers who were paid royalties in gold from that
country, and not just rubles deposited in their name. Undoubtedly these concessions were made with the idea that he would
eventually be won over. In the meantime deviations were over-
looked for the sake of his prestige value. The height of Waldo
Frank's participation in Communist Party activities was his tour
with Earl Browder during the campaign of 1936. Throughout
the relationship, he was trying to convert Communism as much
as the Communists were trying to convert him. He envisioned
what he called "Integral Communism," "to transfigure the
meaning of the word 'communist' in order that the social motive
may integrally derive from a true mystic (cosmic) consciousness
of the person," as he put it in his notebook. He saw Marx as a
mystic—a Hebrew prophet with a fundamental flaw—that his
chosen people, the proletariat, could not sin. By revolution,
Waldo Frank has always meant personal revolution—an activity within the person, creating wholeness in the person. At

the time of the popular front, such heresy could be forgiven by the Communists; but when, during the Moscow trials, Frank wrote a letter critical of their procedure for the *New Republic*, the too-holy alliance was over.

Energies that might have been turned to the novel had instead been turned to social action; yet when the novel did come, it profited from these experiences, including the head-bashing in Kentucky.

11

The Death and Birth of David Markand

THE FIFTY THOUSAND WORDS OF THE NEW NOVEL WRITTEN DUR-
ing the summer of 1927 at St. Georges d'Oléron, now preserved
in a manuscript entitled *The Birth of David Markand*, in the
University of Pennsylvania Library, provide us with an indication of Frank's conception of the novel at an early stage. The
fragment begins some years after the conclusion of *The Dark
Mother* and was evidently intended as a sequel to that work.
David Markand has married Helen, the girl he had finally set-
tled on at the end of the 1920 novel, and they have two children. David's uncle, Anthony Deane, has recently died, and
David is willed a share in his business. An unrest festering in
David is brought to a head by his wife's conversion to Catholicism, and he leaves his home to return to Clearden, the little
town in Connecticut where the earlier novel begins. Seeking
rebirth, he goes back to his birthplace, strives to find himself,
but does not succeed; he eventually is forced to leave because of
his friendship for a neighbor, a widow. A loose sheet in the
manuscript contains an outline, showing that one more section,
involving a place called Centralia, was intended, but the text

goes no farther. Waldo Frank seems to have gone back also, to the style and method of 1920.

On page 3 of Notebook X is the following entry:

> January 12, 1929
> *On Dec.* 31, I was utterly outside the novel. In less than two weeks, I find myself again in it, and it is rapidly transforming by virtue of this contact. Thus the first two parts—(the 50,000 words written in July, 1927) (in St. Georges d'Oléron)—must be overhauled—a whole new dimension must be infused. And the unilateral "portrait" form of the book as a whole has been abandoned. The aesthetic structure of the novel will be radically different from what I had supposed. The subject form, so successful in Rahab and in many City Block stories, is no longer valid for what I feel. More profoundly, the novel will be an organic creation of America   1.
> —whence emerges a Man   2.
> —whence is posited (at the end)   3.
> the fertile juncture (or, at least, the moving toward each other in attraction) of this Man and this America.

But Waldo Frank was not ready to write yet. First came Latin, America, then Russia. On page 51 of the same notebook, written on the ship returning from Russia, Frank recognized that the main question to be answered in the novel had not been answered for him before he visited Latin America and Russia. A child of the middle class, enjoying its luxuries and considering them necessities, yet sympathizing with the "still unspoiled human world—the child, the worker, the peasant," he still had to make his choice—and that choice would be reflected in the life of David Markand. From his middle class island, on the Upper West Side of the Island in the Atlantic, he had looked both ways, and had chosen America rather than Europe; but he had remained in the cultural isolation of the middle class, insulated from the problems of society that he next wanted to write about.

On his return from Russia he felt that he had decided what he should do; therefore he knew what the outcome of his novel should be. First he must express, however, what he had experienced in Russia, and in three months—until the first of February, 1932—he drafted *Dawn in Russia.*

On February 6, he wrote the following in his notebook:

On Threshold of the Novel.

I am not certain that it is wise to develop the lines of the complete & detailed action fully, in the abstract, before writing—although this was my method in the past. There is a danger, that by so doing the action of the characters may be somewhat arbitrary—& their form, in consequence, too intellectual & unconvincing. Possibly, for profound creation, something of improvisation is needed. . . .

I am on the point of a brief visit to the miners of Kentucky in the great strike. I expect, primarily, to win of this, the renewed *taste* of America. On my return, a couple of speaking dates—& then I must bravely shut myself away & begin to write.

He did not. The Kentucky incident brought on many speaking engagements, so that he did not return to the novel until he went to the Saratoga artists' colony, Yaddo, on May 12. Even there, he devoted himself to practice on the 'cello and the rereading of Spinoza, only gradually getting started on the novel. With some interruption, the work continued for almost two years, the first draft being completed on July 14, 1933, and revision taking until February of the following year. The book was published October 8, 1934.

As indicated by the note made before his journey to Latin America, Frank had reorganized the novel completely. The first two parts cover the same actions as those in the St. Georges d'Oléron manuscript, but they are better motivated and on a grander scale. His intention is expressed more explicitly on page 89 of Notebook X:

This book is the story of the Birth of a Man—of a true *person*. David Markand's life, in I, is the passive result of Helen & of Deane & Co. He stirs from this: going back to self, he becomes—must remain for a while—more passive. This is II—the Mother & the Village. He is driven forth with Sarah who is surrogate to his mother. *The River* (III) marks the period of his "adolescence"— (Wanderjahre): in which he confronts crucial problems in himself: Sex, Art, Revolution, Business—& solves them severally thus preparing for a central mastery. These problems come to D., socially as he enters various groups or communities of people: & into relations with various persons. And, having finally touched everything in that way, from the Kentucky mines to Europe, he goes back to Home—in N. Y: & self, then—years of dying & re-birth, deep down, while (by counterpoint) the world swirls about him. And emerges the true place, Clearden, the true person, Markand.

In its execution, this plan underwent dramatic condensation that is reflected in the title change from *The Birth of David Markand* to *The Death and Birth of David Markand*. Before the birth of the Person, the old Markand had to die—the Markand who, like Waldo Frank, was tied closely to the middle class. Markand may have succeeded, but since Waldo Frank's success was less definite, Markand's became blurred and full of paradoxes. Moreover, since this novel, like *The Dark Mother* and *Rahab*, is the seeking out of a method, it has in it mingled but not blended almost all the older styles of Waldo Frank, with occasionally a new style blossoming forth. Although he had decided to abandon the unilateral form, he had not fully developed what was to replace it, and so the unilateral shows through too often.

I construe Frank to mean by *unilateral* the concentration of the lyric novels on the person. In abandoning it, he was striving to include society into his schema. The large-scale structure that he envisioned for his second phase of novel writing developed in *The Death and Birth of David Markand* as the second lyric form developed in *Rahab*. At first, he did not know what to call the structure he was trying to create. While the novel was in the making, he referred to the series as the epics. By the time he completed his plans for the second such work, *The Bridegroom Cometh*, he called them the symphonic novels.

Although it may have been suggested by Huxley's use of the term, either in *Point Counterpoint* or as referred to by Beach, in *The Twentieth Century Novel*, that he read about this time, reference to "counterpoint" in the note quoted above indicates that Frank's thinking about the novel was coming to be in terms of music. The aptness of the title *symphonic*, however, is much more evident in *The Bridegroom Cometh*. This book divides into two main parts, the first beginning with one unsatisfactory harmony and ending in another, an unsatisfactory resolution of the protagonist's problems, achieved through disintegration of the first. The second part brings about a further disintegration and concludes with a resolution that has the ring of finality. Like a symphony, it moves from a harmony with possibility of further development through chaos to completed harmony.

In *The Death and Birth of David Markand* the overall structure is not this neat. Although the novel progresses through the creation of a person who seems to have found his place as a part of the whole of things, we are not sure what solution that person has found or will find for the problems of existing as an effective member of his society; and in the context of the novel, the person and society are linked. Not only must David Markand make himself aware of God without destroying himself as a part of society, but he must act to make his society one that will, without destroying itself, include God. At the end, David seems to be capable of attacking the question; but what he will do remains uncertain.

Both novels, however, like symphonies, trace the development of several themes in counterpoint. The "saint and sinner" themes of *The Dark Mother* are continued, Tom Rennard becoming more of a rascal as David moves toward sainthood. And in addition to the themes of the characters, various themes represent America: business and crime, religion and radicalism, sexual satisfaction and frustration, wealth and poverty. The most effective use of the analogy of symphonic music is in making the themes of America the themes also of David Markand. If throughout the novel this integration could have been carried out as well as it was in the last two parts, the form would have been as successful in the earlier work as it was in *The Bridegroom Cometh*; but in the first two sections there was too much derivation from *The Dark Mother*.

In Book One, "Deane and Company," motivations are given for David's fundamental act of quest, but some of the subordinate acts remain obscurely motivated. The problem of motivation is a profoundly difficult one; David is the passive result of two influences, his wife and the job his uncle gave him, and the next step, according to Frank's plan, is for him to break away, go back to his mother's home, and endure a period of greater passivity. Breaking away seems to be possible only through his not remaining passive—how then must he accomplish the transition? It is done neatly and convincingly in the novel. David awakens one morning in his East Side house, a home he had no part in creating. It was a wedding gift from his father-in-law and all the furnishing was planned by his wife, Helen. She is already up, dressing to go out; she has been getting up before him and going out alone many mornings. Her very act, and its secrecy, plants alienation within him. He thinks of his work, since he is in it purely because of his uncle, whose will is to be read that day. He thinks of the merger of Deane and Company with United Tobacco Industries, successfully accomplished on Deane and Company's terms because of his uncle's reluctance toward the merger. Thus discontent is added to disinterest in the lineup of motivations.

At the reading of the will he discovers he is an heir on equal footing with Anthony Deane's own children—and he is singled out with the privilege of withdrawing from the company. Having foreseen that David might not want to continue as a businessman, (this is not in the 1927 St. Georges d'Oléron version) his uncle pointed the way he should go by leaving to him the house that belonged to his mother, in Clearden, Connecticut. Thus when his wife tells him she has been converted to Catholicism, providing a spiritual support in his absence, the way is clear for him. He turns the management of his estate over to his old friend, Tom Rennard, and leaves his home.

Many of the later themes are sounded in this portion. As David sits at the breakfast table with his children, for example, before the will-reading, looking at the Sunday paper, the headlines make him think only of the details of his self-sufficient life. Before the end of the book, however, he will be a part of the forces that make such headlines. One of them is: "Strike Violence in Patterson [sic]. Paul Wood Jailed." Paul Wood will set in motion a train of events that will mean blows on the body of David Markand and the death of two of his friends; but as yet that David Markand is not born. One of the inducements for David to stay with the business is a coming business coup— a monopoly on the output of a ranch in Vera Cruz where a very superior tobacco can be grown at low cost. One member of the firm, commenting on the price, asks, " 'How can they do it?' . . . 'That's their business,' smiled Sanders. Sobel chuckled. 'I suppose they can make those peons work for even *less* than nothing.' " Then follows a counterpoint passage:

. . . That afternoon, while the two big men of UTI studied the Dolores papers, a peon on the Dolores ranch in the State of Vera Cruz, having stolen a purse that contained five silver pesos from the foreman, and having attempted to escape with his wife and children to another village, stood in a dug hole within the fallow tobacco field, with only his head above ground and all his body buried. Four mounted guards lined up in single file, about twenty feet be-

tween them, and spurred their horses. They were expert riders, and
the hoofs of each horse struck the peon's head. Before the last one
passed, the peon's shattered skull sagged to the earth and his
mouth poured blood. Three brother peasants dug the dead body
and laid it in holy ground, wrapping the mangled skull in a white
scarf that instantly turned crimson, while a priest prayed. For this
holy service, the three peasants paid the priest a silver peso. And
that night, the priest will drink his peso in *tequilla* at the same
tavern table with the mounted guards who, also, have been paid in
silver for doing their duty.

Between the scenes at the UTI offices and in Vera Cruz,
David's wife Helen is shown kneeling in prayer in a church near
the poorer section of the East Side, praying for "constant closeness to her fellow men and women, to understand them as she
did her children, and to help them." Beside her is a woman
whose son needs an operation, praying for the money to pay
for it. The two women arise together, and Helen smiles at the
other and might have perceived from her troubled expression
that the woman was wishing for money rather than a smile.
"But Helen, despite her closeness to all men and women, did
not hear her."

As can be seen from these examples, counterpoint in the
opening section produces an almost editorializing use of irony.
There are other "old-style" variations from the direct story line,
some of them even more reminiscent of *The Dark Mother*.
After the will reading, David almost pointlessly has intercourse
with Lois, the cousin he was physically attracted to in the
earlier novel. This may be to complete unfinished business, to
show David's passivity, or to mark estrangement with his wife.
He picks up a showgirl, gives her dinner and a hundred dollars,
but finds then that he does not have the inclination to sleep
with her. Again and again he finds himself incapable of carrying
out a sexual experience, the only apparent motivation that he

is capable of having normal intercourse again only after his "birth."

This kind of episode when mingled with the unanimistic side-flashes of the intersection of society and the life of David Mark-and seems unreal, for they operate at different levels of perception. If the total effect is unified and the reader is sufficiently prepared, symbolic episodes can be made real actions as they are in *City Block* and *Holiday*. But when these episodes appear in a context of naturalistic dialogue and action, or side-by-side with indignation aroused by irony, as in the Vera Cruz episode, they seem out of place. It is true that the mystical-lyrical-erotic passages are considerably modified from their earliest form in Waldo Frank's writing, but if they are to be blended with propaganda or social criticism, both they and the propagandistic passages must be modified. Helen prays, but her prayer is not answered; it seems more logical as well as effective ironically that it not be answered. But if Helen cannot find truth without motivation, David must be motivated in his discovery of truth, as much in the contrapuntal episodes as he is in the main stream of the novel; and the counterpoint increases as the novel proceeds.

Although Book Two, "The Mothers," contains more of the earlier sort of passages, it is more effective than Book One, for it standing alone has many of the ingredients of a complete lyric novel. David returns to Clearden, now almost a ghost town, and creates a turbulence in the lives of a number of people: Deborah Gore, who cooks for him, and in whom he finds a substitute mother; Stan Poldiewicz, a Polish immigrant farmer who was once a chef and his wife Christine, a girl from a Kansas farm; Lucy Demarest, who tries to make David her lover and acts, with Deborah's son, in having David run out of town. They are made from the same pattern as Virginia and Bob Hade in *Holiday*. While the turbulence is growing, David seeks out his roots, reads his father's papers, remembers his

mother. A lyrical passage develops the idea that the life of
David in the city was no life, that he died in a way when his
parents died, and goes on to say, "You will have no being . . .
Until desire is born within you. . . ."

The least unified part of the novel is Book Three, "The
River," which breaks down into several parts: "The Prairie,"
"Helen," "Pastoral," "The City," and "The Gulf." "The Prairie"
contains David's experiences in Centralia, Kansas, working at
various jobs and dropping constantly in the economic scale.
He learns, by working at an illegal bar, that illegal business does
not differ from legal, and he senses the immorality in the business practices he formerly had disliked vaguely. He is at first
amused by the job: "Then tobacco, now booze—both things
meant to make life pleasant. One, legal; one in this state illegal.
It didn't make much difference. Cigars paid an excise tax to
the government; booze paid a graft tax to the men who ran the
government. . . . It was closer to the life of business, it was
truer." But when he learns that his son has died, and goes to
identify himself at the bank, get money to return to New York
and put things back the way they had been, he finds that the
bank president is the "big boss" of the speakeasy syndicate, the
man who takes rakeoffs from prostitutes, the center of the web
he had amusedly compared with his former life. The evil he
had been trying to escape embodied for him, he could neither
go back to his job nor to New York and his former life. Out
of work, he goes from poor quarters to poorer ones, and close to
starvation, accepts charity from his Negro landlady, saying, "You
shouldn't feed me. . . . I'm your enemy. I got two hundred
thousand dollars."

In a contrapuntal passage we learn that Stan Poldiewicz, having left Clearden to work as a chef in New York, following the
mob scene of David's departure at the end of Book Two, was
injured in a strike and then cast off by the union. He dies,
muttering "Man is bad." This leaves Christine free to be at her

brother's in Kansas when David arrives there, after a walk across the prairie in flight from the personified evil of Centralia. During his walk he fell in with some IWW workers and comes to the realization that in dynamiting a struck mine they were using violence against violence and were neither better nor worse than the operators.

"The Prairie" ends with David's arrival at Philip Dwelling's house in Melleville, the setting of "Pastoral." Before the opening of "Pastoral," however, the section called "Helen" takes us back to David's wife in New York, at confession. Her artificial acts of penance contrast ironically with the ordeal David has imposed on himself. Just as capitalism and unionism which uses the methods of capitalism are rejected in "The Prairie," the progressivism of the Farmer's League, a symbol for the Non-Partisan League, is rejected in "Pastoral." David works out a law of power: "Live for power, in terms of fame or money, and you stink. . . . Try to live without power, and you die. . . . There's something more to this 'law' . . . a third clause we haven't got hold of."

The main theme through these sections, the first part of Book Three, is David's political development. Much less clear and convincing through these parts is his spiritual and emotional development, symbolized erotically, and indicated by something akin to impotence. David seems to be physically capable of coitus, but incapable of love. He hurts everyone who helps him. He rejects every woman who makes herself available to him save one, a prostitute in Centralia, with whom he has intercourse as an act of hate. Other themes are introduced, but they seem to be fragments not related to David, although they serve an important function in describing the state of the nation.

As we have seen before, where the syllable "Mark" appears, there is Waldo Frank. Projected into other terms, the story of David Markand is his story. The quest of David Markand for himself—his trying to find himself as a person—through physical ordeals, corresponds with Waldo Frank's quest through spiritual ordeals. But *The Death and Birth of David Markand*, as can be seen from the title, is not just a quest; it is also a flight. David is also fleeing the middle class. Two steps in the development of a consciousness of the class struggle correspond almost exactly between Waldo Frank and David Markand: in 1914, in Book Three, David's work with the Farmer's League echoes Waldo Frank's work with the Non-Partisan League in 1914. In 1917, in Book Four, David is assaulted for siding with strikers in "Howton," Kentucky; in 1932 Waldo Frank was assaulted for the same reason in Harlan, Kentucky. But Waldo Frank did not put himself to the trials of poverty that David does in Book Three, and unlike David, he did not cast off all connection with the middle class. That is the trouble with David as a convincing character. He has, outwardly, turned entirely away from the society he formerly belonged to; but because his real-life image, Waldo Frank, had not done that, David does not do it convincingly. What more bourgeois attitude than that of providing lasting comfort and security for one's family! And David is very careful to do so. Frank exploits this irony by counterpointing time after time the development of David as a force for good, while one of David's adjuncts, his wealth, is wielded by a scoundrel as a force for evil. When he tells the poor Negro family whose food he is eating, "You shouldn't feed me. . . . I'm your enemy. I got two hundred thousand dollars," his knowledge of the class struggle is symbolized, but we still wonder why he doesn't telegraph Tom Rennard for some money and buy his benefactors a basket of groceries. It is logical that he should not take the conscience-soothing method of charity; but it does not ring true emotionally.

Central to the section "The City," and central to the entire novel, is the symbolic death and birth of David. He becomes a stockyard worker in Chicago, taking a room in the poor house of Juan and Marita Fierro. After some period of time he falls ill. The doctor says it is exhaustion and the heat, and recommends a diet that for the Fierros is impossible. Juan brings a priest, and when David awakens to find him there, he shouts, "Not the priest. Not Helen!" He clutches at Marita, and Juan tells her to give him what he needs. What he needs, and what she gives, is not at all clear, and perhaps should be less so. There is a symbolism with her breast that at its most obvious interpretation would seem to indicate David as the newborn child. It marks the turning-point, at any rate, both in David's illness and in his development into a Person.

On recovery he meets again Theodora Lenck, wife of a meat packer, whom he had met when he first arrived in Chicago, and they go off together to the Wisconsin woods. He seems almost a child to her—will not talk, seems to have no interest in the ideas and art that interest her. Theodora resolves to make him over, and a Montessori school she sponsors in Alabama occurs to her as a good place to do it.

It would occur to any reader who did not try to follow the symbolism that David's experience with the Fierros and his time as a laborer in the stockyards is merely an interruption to the influence of Theodora on his life. A writer disinterested in mysticism and in symbols would probably omit it entirely, and be satisfied with the result. Without it, the mental and physical development of David would be demonstrated just as well. It is, in other words, an episode from a novel like *Rahab* put into a different sort of book. Without doubt, the function of the episode in the purpose of Waldo Frank is essential, however. He is not engaged in a psychological study; he had ceased limiting himself to psychology fifteen years before. It is important, but in the context of his new sort of novel, it is not convincing.

It was necessary for the author to mark somehow David's spiritual discovery. The death and birth scene does not do this effectively; but to see better what it does say, and perhaps to catch a glimpse of the flaw in the method, we need to consider

what, in 1932-4, Waldo Frank felt was the kind of religious feeling David Markand should have.

God, Frank wrote in his notebook then, is the principle of
unity in the multiverse. In Christianity and Buddhism, he
believed, knowledge of God means destruction of the world
and the self, for in a world where survival is an instinctive,
unconscious action, knowledge of God is self-destruction. Only
the one who has, by means of science, substituted conscious
for unconscious action in survival can know God without en-
dangering his survival. This means whereby individuals can know
God and survive seems to have something in common with
certain forms of Hinduism, where the science is a conscious
control of the normally unconscious life actions—breathing,
digesting, etc. For a group (such as the America that is co-
protagonist with David in the novel) there must be corporate
consciousness that disposes of instinctive action for knowledge
of God and survival at the same time. Men, therefore, must not
be at the mercy of the forces they themselves create, as well as
not being at the mercy of natural forces. Frank comments that
all groups needing to survive, yet living on the instinctive, unconscious level, have rejected God, either by creating a false god
who is really the projection of their instinctive ego, or by
destroying God altogether.

Somewhat earlier, before starting on the novel, Frank wrote:

> The interpretative quest and the answer are within man, hence
> God is within man. This quest and answer are essences of man's
> existence (called activities of his spirit or mind), hence God is
> within the essence of man's existence. God, as man's experience, is
> lodged in his activity and is of the traits and forms of his essence.
> Man must therefore seek God within self whence all his experi-
> ence of nature wondrously distils that experience of which nature
> itself cannot be the form: the experience of God. . . .
> This quest and finding, in man's self, of God is a composition of
> man's activities brought to a certain pitch of unitary consciousness.

Both the quest and the finding are indissoluble from the activities of the man: there is no abstract or absolute true search and finding of God. . . .

The flaw now seems evident. A mystical experience takes place through a seeking within man for God; it is the emergence of consciousness onto another plane, and a description of externals, however symbolic, except as transformed within the consciousness that is aware of God, cannot communicate the finding to one who has not experienced it. Even so, each man finds God in his own way, and many do not find God at all. The symbol, which for Waldo Frank and perhaps for one who has found God in ways like Waldo Frank's could be a vital and effective one, remains a dead symbol to those who have not had analogous experiences. On the smaller scale of the lyric novel, where the development up to the moment of truth can be kept closely in mind and where atmosphere, unbroken because of brevity, makes apocalypses real, Frank had found his technique. For certain readers, even in *The Death and Birth of David Markand*, he could use a similar technique. But for the reader at large, another technique would need to be found. Even the most un-mystical, however, can follow the further development of David into a Person, since for Waldo Frank the finding of God is a continuous process.

In "The Gulf," David's re-education is begun by Theodora and continued by Lida Sharon, a radical teacher, as David rejects Theodora's liberalism and even gets started reading Marx. In Book Four, "The Mountain," this education is picked up by John Byrne, with whom David wanders across the South. "The Mountain" contains some of the best and some of the worst of the novel. It is a kind of picaresque tale, with much of the unexplainable coincidence common to that type, but it succeeds in creating the effect of a dynamic society as background to David far better than any of the preceding sections.

Its effective counterpoint begins with Helen, reading the newspaper in her home and receiving a letter from David. She keeps the letter until last, like a sybaritic child eating the cake first and then settling down to the icing, and as she begins her orgy of words, we shift to John Byrne, a radical, not far from Helen's house, who has just received a letter from the same Paul Wood who figured in a headline in the opening of the novel, and who was among the IWW men David met in Kansas. Wood's letter suggests that Byrne go South. "If we can get the IWW ideology into their heads before the mills bust their nerve, we'll start the revolution down there." His thoughts run back, and we learn that he came to his present situation by way of being a follower first of Daniel DeLeon, then of Debs; going to Germany and being influenced by Rosa Luxemburg, returning at her request to work for the revolution here. We shift to Theodora, who has left the school for Hollywood, displeased with her life. We shift to Lida Sharon, in Alabama, writing to Byrne, suggesting that if he gets South, he visit her.

Simultaneous with news of Theodora's suicide is the arrival of John Byrne at the school. Those two things lead David to go with him when Byrne leaves, and they hike through Alabama, sleeping in barns and working for their meals. At one farmhouse, they are treated coldly, but fed after they cut stove-wood, and unbeknownst to the farmer they sleep in his barn. During the night the farmer's daughter takes refuge in the barn from her sexually-aroused father, and they urge her to accompany them. The girl, Jane Priest, is religious, and she and Byrne, the atheist, argue as they fall in love, and David between them absorbs faith from both. They go to Kentucky to take part in a strike of miners.

The strike episode is one of the most effective in the book, and it ends with the same sort of experience that Frank underwent in Harlan. Jane and Byrne are both killed, however, while David, injured, escapes. It is the penultimate step in the development of David Markand, the whole person. He is still more observer than participant, as Waldo Frank was in Kentucky, but he takes all the risks that the participants do. He has become a man of great moral strength, of presence, and it is his action in attempting to save Byrne's life that saves his, since he is knocked unconscious and is not seen in the dark.

The dénouement contains some of the organic irony of Frank's earlier books, transposed effectively to the larger scale of this one. Tom Rennard comes to Washington, lawyer for the steel company David's money is invested in. Having access to confidential information, he learns that the United States is about to enter the war; yet he decides that now he has multiplied David's fortune, he will take it out of steel, since Helen will disapprove of making money from munitions, and it will be evident to her now that the materials of war are the basis of the accumulation to her funds. Tom is so well off, and has brought David's inheritance to such a figure, that he can overlook the possible stock market killing in his advance information, but tosses it as a tip to his assistants.

David, by this time arrived in Washington after wandering from the Kentucky border, has decided finally to go home. Through calling Tom's office in New York he learns that he is in Washington, and starts for his hotel. On the way, after walking through the tide of newsboys calling "WAR," he goes into a Negro restaurant and eats soup, knowing that he cannot pay for it. This is the second test of whether he should return or not. The first time, when he learned of his son's death in Centralia, he realized that it was not yet time. Now he sets another test in the way, since the woman who runs the restaurant will take sexual intercourse in place of money. So while Tom waits in his hotel, David goes to bed with the shabby proprietress. The question is which world is properly his, that of the Negro, of the lower classes, of another symbolic death; or the world that would come of taking a cab to Tom's hotel.

He chooses the cab, and the book ends, not as originally planned, with David at rest in Clearden, but with David taking a taxicab toward life.

The ending is not so conclusive, but it is more vital than the one originally planned. The old David Markand has died, and a new one has been born and has grown up. He has chosen life, but he has not done anything with it yet. He has still not found the answer to the riddle of power—between the corruption that Tom symbolizes, and the death that the Negro woman symbolizes, he has chosen another course—but we are not told what that course is, except that it is neither of the others:

> Markand leaned forward in the cab, a large body of a man in a corduroy suit and a gray flannel shirt and a rough slouch hat, riding through the stratified death of Washington.

The image clearly is of a new Walt Whitman, dressed in the old clothes, but in Washington at a new war.

> The shudder in his body, he knew, was only a beginning. The shudder must grow, the shudder must multiply, the shudder must rage, within the body of the world. It must quake down the empty buildings, it must grind down the grinding institutions, it must turn the tide of men streaming to death back to their source, which is life. . . .
> He knew, while his body trembled, that he loved Helen and she was still his wife: he would love, when again he knew them, his children.
> —Are their lives of this stratified death, of this enemy Body I must help destroy? He knew that it was so.

It is possible that all along Waldo Frank had not intended this novel to end on a definite conclusion, even though one is suggested in the note outlining it in Notebook X, with David finding his place in Clearden. As far back as 1922 he planned three volumes of sequel to *The Dark Mother*, the whole series to be called *Men and Dreams*. At first the sequence was to be *The Dark Mother, David, Thomas* (children of the Dark Mother), and *The Way of Mary*. *Mary*, which was apparently at least suggested by the unpublished novel "The Sisters," was to symbolize the Dark Mother. Gradually the character of Tom Rennard became less interesting to Frank, and his concept of Mary changed, until the plan evolved into a book about Mary, and one about David and Mary together, in addition to the ones already done. The ending in Clearden, then, could have been an extension into one of the sequels, rather than a planned ending for this novel. It is difficult to say, for as Waldo Frank changed, so did his concept of his books. We shall, before we are through, take David, in another guise, into rural retirement.

There is a lack of harmony between form and content in *The Death and Birth of David Markand*, and there is a flaw in the characterization of David. As we have seen, like *Rahab*, it contains a groping for a method. In addition, although it says that David Markand the middle class entity has died, and David Markand the unattached person has been born, we are not convinced that any such thing has happened. In the end, David Markand is spiritually and emotionally a person, it is true, but the development of that person has been by mysterious and often unmotivated actions; the significance of each step is not clear to us. The convincingness of the result, and unconvincingness of the process, results from Frank's not having achieved his method, the symphonic style, uniformly through the book. The economic person, David Markand, on the other hand, is convincingly developed, but we cannot believe in the result. He does not really escape from the middle class, because Waldo Frank, with his more substantial background of the uniform brownstone rows of the Upper West Side and a quite satisfactory childhood in them, had not escaped from the middle class. Frank's adherence to middle class values makes inconsistencies in David's actions; he disapproves of bourgeois ethics, but he adheres to them absolutely. In the end, David decides not to become a part of the class he is dedicated to. Instead, he will keep his money and the power his money gives him, and, we can imagine, exercise a position of leadership in the revolutionary movement. The book does not say so. It reflects the ambivalent position of Waldo Frank, who was at that time simultaneously opposing and following middle class standards; we cannot criticize his personal decision to do so, but we cannot help being dissatisfied with the ambivalence that decision gives to the conclusion of his novel.

12

The Bridegroom Cometh

THE CHANGE THAT CAME ABOUT IN WALDO FRANK'S CONCEPTION of his series of symphonic novels did not result purely from changes in his ideas. His first marriage had ended in divorce, and in 1927 he married Alma Magoon, a New England girl who had been brought up in a dour family of fundamentalist religious views, from which she had deviated as had Frank from the religious liberalism of his father. Alma symbolized for Waldo Frank the old tradition in America and the change it underwent. Therefore as the old plan of the David Markand novels faded from his interest, it was replaced by the idea of tracing, in the next volume, the story of Alma projected into symbolic terms as his own story was projected in *The Death and Birth of David Markand*. The fourth volume, then—or, since he came gradually to consider *The Dark Mother* as an honorable failure, the third—was to be of the marriage of David with Mary, the symbol for Alma. Since Alma was for him America, the symbolism and solution posited in the beginning would be carried out effectively—the marriage of the prophet and America, the person and the people.

As soon as *The Death and Birth of David Markand* was completed, he began to plan a schedule for writing its sequel. The schedule and the basic plan were altered, however, by events in Frank's life. First of all, the proposed next volume needed much more preparation than he imagined. He planned to begin

149

writing in May, 1935, after a visit to Manchester, N. H., to get background for the opening part. He went to his house in Truro, Massachusetts, to begin writing, but soon after was called to the Writers Congress and was elected head of the League of American Writers. By June he was in Paris, invited by Rolland, Gide, and Malraux to the International Congress of Writers. From there he went to England, not returning to America until August.

After a long period of consolidation in his mind of the materials of the book, writing and revision of scenarios, and pondering on Marx and religion, he set to work determined not to let himself be pulled away for anything. With difficulty he lived up to his resolution, even when civil war broke out in Spain; he wrote in his notebook that no loyalty, concern, or interest must interrupt, and from December, 1935, to September, 1936, he completed the first draft. Since it is his practice to let a cooling off period intervene between first writing and revision, he closed the Truro house and engaged again in action. His first concern was Spain, and he set aside even personal problems to do what he could for the Spanish Loyalist Government. In addition he accompanied Earl Browder, Communist Party candidate for the presidency of the United States, on his campaign tour. He had originally planned to visit Russia that fall, but, he wrote on page 176 of Notebook XII, "Spain has cancelled Russia." He prepared for the press a collection of essays, planned somewhat earlier with the help of Harold Clurman, that was published by Farrar & Rinehart in 1937 with the title *In the American Jungle.*

As early as the beginning of 1937 he saw the possibility that democracy in Spain would be ground out of existence between the Fascists and the Communists, so when he was invited to attend the Congress of Writers and Artists in Mexico, he accepted, knowing that he would probably be invited to talk with Leon Trotsky. He had for some time been losing faith in the possibility of cooperation with the Communists, and he felt Stalin's arch-enemy would have a point of view worth hearing. The Moscow Trials were then under way, and as a test of how much deviation would be permitted him, he proposed, in a letter to the New Republic, the formation of an international tribunal as a court of appeal for the old bolsheviks. A heated reply by Earl Browder set off a mass of controversy, and the period of cooperation between Waldo Frank and the Communist Party was ended. Although frequently interrupted by such things, Frank worked on revision of his novel until the fall, when the entire family moved to England, where Alma had arranged to study under F. Matthias Alexander. There clearly was also a suppressed wish in Waldo Frank's soul to see Spain in crisis.

In September the Franks arrived in London. Since revision of the book did not seem to progress favorably, by the end of the month Waldo Frank decided to visit Spain. The catalysts that set off creation are hard to locate, and they seem to be operative only when the writer has his materials finally in shape in his subconscious. Moreover, if he does not act when the materials are in shape, he seems to have the whole job to do over again. We have seen frequently in this study the long periods of gestation necessary for the creation of a novel, the false starts and times when no start at all is possible. Suddenly, however, things become right, and the words flow out. In October Frank went to Paris and made all arrangements for his trip into Spain. Then, a few hours before departure time, he suddenly returned to England, and within a week was deep in the revision of the novel, working almost continuously until April, 1938, when it was finished, typed, and copies sent to publishers in the United States and London. In Notebook XIII, pp. 37-44, he speculates at length on why it was he did not go to Spain, attributing to himself everything from cowardice to a headache, but with the help of hindsight it seems obvious that his mind had solved the problem of the novel, shoving the unsolved (and apparently unsolvable) problem of Spain to the background. Late in April he went to Spain, spent three weeks there, and clarified his ideas, not only about the Spanish situation, but about Communism in general. He was attacked in the Communist papers, while Spanish leaders, including the Communists, were friendly toward him. Many years later, in Argentina, he met the man who had been assigned the job of killing him while he was visiting the front, but who had found the job impossible because there were too many among the ranks of the Spanish Communist Party who held Frank in high esteem, and continued to do so in spite of attacks on him in the Communist press.

The Bridegroom Cometh was published in London (by Gollancz) on October 24, 1938, after Frank had returned to the United States. It was not published in his own country until May, 1939.

Many things had changed since the book was first thought of, and most of the changes took place between the first draft and the revision, enabling us, by examination of the manuscript and comparison of it with the final form, to see what effect the changed events had on Frank's conception of the novel. The era of hope for the revolutionary movement ended; his former idealization of his wife naturally suffered some disillusionment, and illness as well as emotional conflict disturbed the relationship; Spain and the entire European world that Frank loved was going to pieces. Fortunately, his conception of the book was one which took only the universals from the political orientation, the person, and the world in which it was set. By the time he had finished the book, Frank realized that the main character, Mary Donald, was not Alma. A reverse Pygmalion, he had made his artistic creation from a human being, and then was just a bit shocked to discover that what he had created was not identical to the woman he married. We, having the advantage of looking back at his method of creating characters impersonally and with forty years of perspective, see nothing at all surprising in that occurrence, since he had been creating projections of his own character all that time, creations that did not correspond with the original. In the act of creation, moreover, he became more like some of his projections of himself, or at least experimented through them with possible developments in himself, while his wife led an existence entirely separate from that of the character in the novel. Mary develops steadily through the book, undisturbed by the separate development of Alma.

Somewhat more surprising, on the surface, is the lack of ambivalence in the book toward the revolutionary movement. When most of the writers for revolution separated themselves from the organization for revolution, they rejected violently all they had previously stood for. A comparison of the finished novel with the first-draft manuscripts in the University of Pennsylvania Library reveals no such reversal in this book, however, and the reason seems quite clear. Frank never was an orthodox Marxist or a follower of revolutionary discipline. Instead he engaged constantly in an attempt to reform the revolutionary movement, and when the great party-line shift occurred in 1937, it was the Communist Party of the United States that changed its position, not Waldo Frank. From being an organization he could hope to reform, and one that was tolerant of those who deviated, providing they were prominent enough, it became more strongly an organ of Russian nationalism, flaunted its dogmatism, and clamped down its discipline. Mary Donald's rejection of party membership, moreover, is a part of the draft Waldo Frank wrote before he went electioneering for the Communist Party candidate for the presidency; it was inevitable in the esthetic logic of the book.

The truly important development in Waldo Frank's fiction at this point is the structural change between *The Death and Birth of David Markand* and *The Bridegroom Cometh*. The

symphonic technique was utilized to the point of unifying sociology and psychology—the people and the person—in the novel.
The interweaving of the themes of groups and individuals, of
movements and ideas; the use of hymns, headlines, popular
songs and slogans, not separate from the identities and actions
of the characters but as parts of their lives, overcomes both
the artificial interruption of the action while a character reads
a newspaper or discusses a current topic, as happens in The
Dark Mother and The Death and Birth of David Markand,
and the arbitrary separation of the stories of the characters from
each other and from the interludes in Dos Passos's U.S.A.
Dos Passos's characters are treated, for the most part, as individuals, as entities, while Frank's are persons, interlinked in
a whole, living in the atmosphere of each other as well as of
the nation.

Frank's hitherto unsolved problem of the clash between natural, interesting dialogue, revealing of character, and the sus-
taining of atmosphere for spiritual development is solved by
dividing the materials into a very close approximation of musical
themes. Mood can be built within a theme, even though it is
entwined with another theme that produces an entirely different
effect. The best illustration of the success of this method is in
Mary's equivalent to the "birth" at the Fierro's of David Mark-
and. The end of her middle class marriage is marked by her
submitting to the caretaker of the summer hotel where she
worked as a young girl. The experience, it is true, is not made
a mystical one—it is symbol merely. But unless its communica-
tion is effective, such a symbol could be disturbing of the whole
effect. It is not only the end of her marriage; it is the end of
Mary Donald as the girl who grew up in a fundamentalist home
in a little New England town; and it is the beginning of a time
when she will live for others. All this makes it a natural time
in the development of Mary for her to submit, and a natural
time for the man to ask. When he says at the end, "Thank you,

girl," it is not in the least bit ludicrous, for such an act and such a response are prepared for in the theme of Mary and the theme of the caretaker, and both seem in character reacting as they do when their themes intersect.

A writer puts something of himself in each of his characters. In Waldo Frank's writings, this something operates on two levels: the lesser characters are present as Frank or some projection of Frank sees them; the major characters are projections of Waldo Frank. We have seen what sort of projections Quincy Burt, David Markand, John Mark, and Karl Loer are. It should be equally evident that Samson Brenner, John Cloud, and many of the *City Block* characters are also projections of Waldo Frank: Samson and the others projections of fragments of Waldo Frank —John Cloud the projection of a larger fragment. In the same way the women characters were created. Prior to *The Bridegroom Cometh*, however, there were no female characters in his writings who were whole projections of Frank, save Fanny Luve. This is not to say that the other women in the lyrical novels or the women in *The Death and Birth of David Markand* are not fully developed studies. Rather, they are projections of real women, as seen by Waldo Frank. Cornelia Rennard is apparently an attempt at projection from himself, as is the professor's wife of *The Unwelcome Man*, but each has accumulated to her certain characteristics of possessiveness which would suggest that the projection was not free of influence from women Waldo Frank had known.

Fanny Luve, however, is purely projection from Frank. Any kind of student of human beings becomes aware that each male has a certain number of feminine characteristics, just as each female has some masculinity, and the degree to which each member of a sex has characteristics of the opposite sex varies among individuals. Waldo Frank is not an effeminate man. For Fanny Luve, he projected his feminine characteristics along with certain of his spiritual attitudes that we could call free of sexual identification. The spiritual Fanny Luve comes to life much more effectively than does the feminine Fanny Luve, and this is quite natural, for the spiritual whole of Waldo Frank is greater than his feminine part. In *City Block*, the amount of feminine Waldo Frank that is projected seems negligible; Fanny is a hag, without any function in the book as a woman. She probably was either suggested by some woman Frank saw in his wanderings of the streets of New York or as a reporter (she may have been suggested by one of the women in the Rosenthal-Becker case), or based on what he imagined a ma-dame past her prime and with an interesting history would be like. In *Rahab*, this figure was borrowed for projection of him-self, and therefore it is not surprising that from time to time— as the competent working woman, for example—she suggests, as did her predecessors, the reflection in Frank of a real woman, rather than the projection from Frank of a woman character.

For all that, Waldo Frank is an acute observer of women. As writer, lecturer, public figure on the intellectual and artistic level, he has lived in a woman's world; and since the very nature of his working day makes it solitary, his companionship, lacking men "on the job" with him, contains a larger proportion of home life, which is usually female-oriented. Moreover, he is attractive to women and apparently always has been. With his highly-developed attribute as an observer, and so much oppor-tunity to observe women, he has acquired the power to present vividly a vast variety of women characters. The men among his incidental characters very often are satirized or made the butt of irony; and although he can sharply satirize women also— Mrs. Forbish, the progressive educator in *The Bridegroom Cometh* is a prime example—he treats sympathetically many more women characters than men.

Mary Donald is the strongest and most sympathetically treated of all of Frank's female characters, whole spiritually and whole physically in a way denied to Fanny Luve. How, then, did Frank create her? He began, as we have seen, creating Mary in the image of his wife, Alma. But before he had finished, his attitude toward Alma had changed, and he had discovered that Mary had grown beyond even his first idyllic conception of his wife. Mary is wholly feminine, yet wholly projection of Waldo Frank. How is this possible? To answer this question involves a deeper delving into the creative process than could be substantiated in a work of this scope, but we can at least offer a theory.

Let us consider yang and yin, the opposites that attract each other, each containing within it the germ of the other, and when joined making the whole. There is no novelty in applying the symbols of yang and yin to the male and the female. Man and woman are complementary to one another, each requiring the other for completeness. Without Mary, David Markand was incomplete, or at least ineffective. Without David, Mary certainly was incomplete. Could it be, then, that instead of projecting a part of himself, Frank projected a complement to himself; a complement that completed the projection of himself that is David Markand, one containing opposites of himself. Waldo Frank's background is international, cultured, libertarian, Jewish. Mary's is American (and before that, Anglo-Saxon), lacking in artistic and intellectual culture, authoritarian, fundamentalist. This whole concept is figure of speech, of course, but it has substance in two facts observable in the novel: Mary Donald is a vital, three-dimensional character; and she is capable of making David Markand effective.

By chance or unconscious intent, the woman Waldo Frank chose as his wife at the point when he began to develop in the direction symbolized by David Markand was one with a background complementary to his own. For some period of time, at least in his opinion then, she developed as a complement to him. Whatever divergence from that path was made afterward by Alma Magoon Frank, the facts of her background

up to then were pertinent to the background of a complementary organism to another oganism, projected from the character
of Waldo Frank. Thus it seems possible that Frank made from
his wife's potentialities a complement to his own potentialities.

Tenuous as this theory may be, there can be no doubt of the
organic unity of the character, the method, and the novel. The
themes develop through their relations to one another, from the
leitmotiv of Mary to the booming counterpoint of Armageddon.
And in the ending there is a resolution that echoes the opening,
both in Mary's reaffirmation of faith and recovery of hope, and
in her relationship to the other themes, among them Armageddon. The resolution at the end is a dynamic rather than a conclusive one, like that of many modern symphonies; the classical
composers could resolve their music conclusively, since an age
of faith provided a conclusive answer to life, but modern composers, living in a time that has not found a satisfactory answer,
can do no more than point in the direction in which they think
conclusive resolution will be found. This idea is symbolized, or
rather Frank's variation of it—that the answer is dynamic, leading to new beginnings—through the titles of the seven sections,
or movements: in "The Last Days," there is Do, Re, Mi, and
Fa—four steps in the musical scale to an uneasy resolution; and
in "The Second Coming," Sol, La, and Si, concluding on the
note that leaves the hearer most uneasy, most expectant of the
beginning of the second octave.

Within each movement there is unity and variety, themes
struggling with each other, and the germ of the next movement.
Unity and movement onward are accomplished sometimes by
placing the narrative in the frame of a single short event, and
letting flashbacks show the development up to that event; sometimes by employing continuous narrative in which the opening
and closing have related emotional effects. These two methods
are fundamentally the same, each being a form of poetic return;

in one case, there is a time-place unity, in the other, identity of effect.

In the first section the events that affected her religion occurring both to her and to those around her are related, all in the form of flashbacks set in the frame of the peak moment of Mary's religious fundamentalism—her baptism, at the age of fifteen. Contrapuntal throughout this section is the theme of Armageddon; it is the day war broke out in Europe in August, 1914. Various themes are brought forward, developed briefly, and dropped: Mary's father and grandfather; her stepmother and aunt and their Lancashire background; her mother and grandmother; her sister Martha and Sid Howard, who will in a later section marry Martha; the first stirring of sex in Mary, and conflict in her between her religion and her love of beauty; and her chance at going to college.

Section two describes the beginning of her break with the world she grew up in, during her three years at Winant College, all set in the frame of a lecture on the revolution in Russia, but with a prelude and coda to the frame. The prelude relates the circumstances of the hiring of Doris Granes, a radical, as teacher of sociology; it is she who gives the lecture. The coda shows Mary's determination to go to New York with Doris rather than return to Winant for her last year. The flashbacks trace Mary's progress to the time she entered college, and some of her experiences at college. In these, she gradually shakes off some of her puritanism, moving from doubt of there being sufficient piety in the college to conviction that it is a place of sanctimonious hypocrisy. Previous themes are developed further and new ones are added.

In part three there are several consecutive frames of Mary's experiences in New York, divided by contrapuntal scenes that reflect world events and serve the same function as Dos Passos's "Newsreel" but are more smoothly articulated into the narrative. The first frame shows the excitement of the false Armistice.

Short scenes depict a New York street, a sweatshop, a scene in Harlem, the Stock Exchange, City Hall, the mayor attaching himself to a parade and then leaving it when he hears that the news is not confirmed, and the subway, all in turmoil over the news. In the subway crowd Martha meets Sid Howard, and flashbacks tell us of the events leading up to the departure of each of them from the home town, and what they are doing in New York. We come eventually to Mary, in Latin class at New Amsterdam College at the moment the news is announced. Classes are dismissed, she goes to the apartment of Doris Granes and her husband, where she lives, and at a party that night meets Willem Taess, a Dutch Jew, wealthy and intellectual businessman.

In the next frame the detachment of Mary from the Graneses is motivated, and we are prepared for her attachment to Willem, while contrapuntally, the marriage of Sid and Martha evolves, and it is made evident that Sid is a gangster.

Mary's job with the Parents' Aid Society, where she interviews people who want to adopt children and visits homes in which children have been placed, makes her grope for love that she sees denied to others, and the discovery that her sister underwent an abortion contributes to her eventual decision to marry Willem.

Contrapuntally, the opening "newsreel" of the false Armistice is echoed in two more such sections: one, after Mary first meets Willem, showing people around a news stand late at night, celebrating the false Armistice and celebrating just as much when they learn it is false; the other, a series of headlines and news stories on the Versailles Treaty, beginning "WORLD WAR ENDS!" including comment on the lesser wars that continue, among them the class struggle, and concluding "HISTORY IS BUNK SAYS HENRY FORD." The undertone of Armageddon thus continues.

Mary's married life is covered in two sections, Fa, the last part of "The Last Days," and Sol, the first part of "The Second Coming." In the first, the marriage is shown deteriorating, but held up by various props and the lack of any next step. In the second, the next step is provided (although Mary does not know it yet) and all the old ties in her life are cut. Martha's husband is killed and she commits suicide. Mary's grandmother dies. She visits her father and stepmother and finds that she is as estranged from her husband's world as she is from theirs, and in spite of his visit to dissuade her, she makes an end to their marriage. The turning point is her intercourse with the old caretaker and friend of her grandmother.

The alternative that is offered her but she does not yet recognize comes in a part of the narrative containing the sort of material that formerly was inserted contrapuntally. This closer articulation seems to show Mary's growing awareness of of the world around her—she who as a college student never kept last year's books or remembered Virgil in the following year's course on Lucretius, comes to a first step of awareness at a party at Doris Granes's. Among the guests are two people who will symbolize further steps in her development: Dr. Cariss, the psychoanalyst, and Dolg, the bolshevik. Both are shown as superior people, but Dolg has a faith, and is more vital. The discussion itself is full of pungent comments on Shakespeare that are really comments on England. The situation is hilarious, for the bolshevik's speech, derived in part from a discussion of Shakespeare that appeared in 1936 in *International Literature*, satirizes the party line as much as it does the British, and the psychologist is an active participant because he has just written a monograph on anal erotic symbolism in the Hamlet-Polonius dialogues. In that setting the party line sounds pretty good.

In two scenes with flashbacks, the sixth section shows Mary's becoming a part of Communism, and, in the person of David Markand, it contains the germs of her rejection of its lack of love. While she tries to support herself, we see in counterpoint

the jerry-built prosperity of the twenties. These two blend together as Mary works through a Christmas season in a department store. Finally she seeks out Dolg and is made an organizer
in the E-Lite Collar Company. The narrative is told in flashbacks as an accident occurs—a new employee's fingers are caught
in a machine. A second level of counterpoint shows the problems of the bosses in the company, indicating that it is not the
individual but the system that is wrong.

The injured girl is Lida Sharon, the radical teacher of *The
Death and Birth of David Markand*, and the second frame,
Mary visiting Lida in the hospital, has flashbacks showing her
development and the split in the socialists that resulted in the
formation of the Communist Party in the United States. ("she
sees John Reed march from the hall, she at his side [thinking of
John Byrne], down fetid Halstead street: feeling with her love
of the dead leader the fragrance of spring, the fragrance of dawn
. . . in the new Party!") Another flashback, comprising Mary's
episode with Dr. Cariss, then as his lover, solidifies her connection with the Communists, since she had come to the place
where she could either turn completely to Cariss or to the Party;
and it returns us to Lida, who, it develops, is also an organizer.
The two girls propose to live together.

The last part, Si, revolves around the theme of lack of love,
heartlessness, in the Communist Party. Lida and Mary organize
a school for workers' children, but they call it a "Sunday-school,"
and they base it on development of self-expression. The party
orders the school closed until Lida and Mary have taken the
course at the Workers' School on Agitprop; their school must
be nothing but a propaganda device. Lida and another party
member, Kurt Doll, fall in love, and they are ordered to go as
organizers to the textile strike in Howton—but first they must
marry. The reason for this is revealed to Mary: they are meant
to be killed by the anti-strike forces, and the death of a young
married couple will make effective propaganda even in the "capi-

talist press," while if they are unmarried, the charge of immorality will outweigh the tragedy of their death. Although the name
"Howton" is the same as the symbol for Harlan, Kentucky, in
The Death and Birth of David Markand, and in the novel identified with it, it has obviously become a symbol for the front
line in the class struggle. "There's always a strike at Howton"
is almost a refrain in this section of the book. Mary asks Mark-
and's help in changing the orders, since he has turned up as an
advisor and doer of good deeds for Party members although not
under Party discipline, but he refuses. The Party will not send
Mary with them; thus ends Mary's time with the Party.

Midway in the section is an episode which is doubly interesting. Like Alfred Hitchcock, who makes himself a bit player in
each of his films, Waldo Frank inserted in *The Bridegroom
Cometh* the scene of a lecture he gave at the Rand School in
1922, without identifying himself by name. This lecture, on the
revolution in art and letters, is pointed out by Markand to another, in Mary's presence, and not knowing why, she goes. In
the question period, the lecturer is attacked for having talked
about revolution without mentioning Marx. He can merely re-
peat that to understand a movement "you got to go back" and
find its source. Markand then rises, to some extent Waldo Frank
of 1937 rising to the defense of Waldo Frank of 1922:

> "Folks," he said, "excuse me. This seems to me a quarrel about
> two ways of skinning an animal. . . . One of these men, the one
> out there in the rear, wants to skin his animal so he can eat it. The
> other one, the gentleman on the platform, wants to skin his so he
> can understand it. The one's interested mainly in the meat . . .
> maybe 'cause he's hungry or knows people that are hungry. The
> other is interested in form and beauty. . . .
>
> ". . . I know hunger is real, even today when they say the land's
> booming and President Coolidge and Mr Mellon swear it'll bloom
> on forever. Hunger's real in Vienna, but I'm told they have their
> opera and concerts. Hunger's real in the Soviet Union, thanks to a

crop failure and half a dozen foreign armies; but the theaters are all open and I'm told they're doing great work in the higher mathematics. I'm not a college man like my friend up there, who, I happen to know, went to Harvard; but I've read Marx and Engels, all I could get in English. And I'm damned if I saw any place where they said economics was everything. . . . For that matter," he smiled and half-turned to the lecturer, "even to understand Marx, you got to go back." Laughter. "There were babes long before the class struggle. If economics is the study of the systems of production for exchange, well, mothers were producing and exchanging long before economics. What I'm driving at is, that life comes first. And life comes last. And, although I don't know much about them, that's what art and literature keep saying."

Here is a David Markand, unattached person, whom we can believe in. Even though he emerges, at one point in the novel, from his house on the Upper East Side, in heart as well as in head he has escaped the middle class. Had the ordeal of a world going to pieces and the betrayal of Spain—plus a more active rôle in the revolutionary movement—dislodged Waldo Frank from the middle class? Mary breaks many of the rules of middle class ethics that David, in the previous novel, strictly adhered to. Until Spain, there was hope of making a new world out of the old; and the collapse of the popular front, that drove many revolutionists back into the middle class, could have driven Waldo Frank finally out of the middle class, since he did not reject his earlier position, but only his earlier strategy, and therefore could be said to have progressed as a spiritual revolutionist.

The night of the lecture is also the night that Mary learns of the orders for Lida and Kurt. At a party meeting after their departure, she feels out of place:

She saw the little room full of smoke, heard the radiator spit, looked into the skylight through which now no moon shone. —I feel men, she had thought. Not now. Sorrow, yes; the will to overcome it, yes. But this will knew no man and no woman; it was the child of sorrow and more than sorrow it denied the man and the woman. —*I cannot do it.* In the conflict, Mary grew dizzy; her mind veered to her childhood, to the prayer meetings when men and women also had gathered to save the world of men and women from sorrow . . . denying also in their way the man and the woman. —*How far have I come?* In her head was their song: The Bridegroom Cometh. —There is no Bridegroom.

David Markand is waiting for her outside the meetingplace. They go to an Irish bar, and the scene there is perfectly realistic for its setting, but apocalyptic as the scene in the *City Block* story "John the Baptist." The drunks sitting around the tables come to symbolize the historian of ideas who is at the same time those ideas, the poet, the artist, the prophet, the fundamentalist, the Communist, and each speaks. To the tune of the old hymn telling of the ten virgins who took their lamps and went forth to meet the Bridegroom, played in a dance rhythm, they rise and dance, but collide with one another, blindly, then go on without anger and disturbance, as if they do not see one another. Markand says, "Don't be afraid. . . . They are all gentle people." But in spite of the lack of anger, they hurt one another and bleed.

Thus he has posed the question of the validity of any philosophy not centered on the Person, on men and women, as she questioned the same lack in both fundamentalism and Communism. But she offers a solution:

> "There is a truth you don't know," she said to David Markand.
> "Yes."
> "You know only the truth to be feared . . . like God the Father."
> "Yes."
> "That Truth has a Son . . . not to be feared. It opens one's eyes . . . so gently, David."
> She got up, and he.
> In her loins the world stirred, sweet with her blood . . . huge.

In his eyes, seeing this young woman, was an Answer, infinite,
yet shaped by miracle for his hands and his mouth. The day was at
the window of the room. They felt it there, the dawn, gray and
cold . . . standing together.

For the second time, Waldo Frank had created his form.

13

Summer Never Ends

IN THE YEARS FOLLOWING THE WRITING OF *The Bridegroom Cometh*, Waldo Frank's world was going to pieces. At first he worked hard in causes that he hoped might save it, but after the betrayal of Spain, it was evident to him that there was little more he could do. Events were in train by then that would be more horrible than anything that had happened in Spain, but the time for effective struggle against them had passed. In 1939, threats of war took him to England, since his family was still there, and when the war came he quickly arranged for passage for himself and his two daughters, and sailed in September. He was, at that time, working on a play, but had been much less active in writing since publication of the novel. Toward the end of the year his marriage permanently broke up, and this heightened all his other sorrows.

In spite of the hopelessness of the struggle and his personal difficulties, however, he felt an urgency for action, and buoyed up by his religious vision, in the latter part of 1939 and the early part of 1940 he wrote *Chart for Rough Water*, published by Doubleday that same year. A direct application of the ideas of *The Re-Discovery of America* to the actuality of a world threatened by fascism, *Chart for Rough Water* shows so keen a perception of the dangers inherent, not only in American Isolationism, but in certain brands of Intervention, that it would be easy to forget that it was written in 1940 and to consider it analysis after the fact rather than prognostication. It devastates Isolationism in twenty pages and traces the history of the European conflict from the Thirty Years War in twenty-nine more! Among "The Desperate Remedies" Frank finds Communism nothing more than Russian Nationalism, and traces three stages in fascism—the racketeer stage symbolized by Mussolini; the stage in which fascism becomes a rationale, under Hitler; and the stage of fascized man. This latter, of course, is the same creature that we have come to know as the "new Soviet man" in his Russian ramification. The true danger, Frank finds, is the fascist within us. "Consult your own life:" he says, "the stifled good in you, the starving strength, the thwarted dream. In your character, and your brother's, you will find fears, confusions, frustrations, dwindling faiths and values which, in the transmutation of crisis, become the fuel and the traits of Fascism."

To propose a solution for this problem, Frank traces, in a longer perspective, the history of Western Civilization again, this time in terms of the individual—the isolated will that, gaining strength, must inevitably move toward fascism—in conflict with the Person—"the individual *through whom the Cosmos speaks.*" [Frank's italics] He says, "A society where, not the individual, but *the potential person* is the norm of value, is one in which all intelligence is dedicated intrinsically—one might almost say 'selfishly'—to the public welfare." He considers the war America's chance to develop its potentiality and to continue the Great Tradition in the arts, education, and politics—to base the nation's activities, in other words, on religion. Not the egocentric religion driven by belief in individual immortality, but the sharing of the dynamic nature of the Cosmos, the acting in the knowledge that "The welfare of his brothers is part of his existence; salvation has no reality outside existence," is the religion whereby fascism could be deflected within us and without.

Frank says:

To destroy Fascism by a frontal war *alone* [my italics] is hopeless, for the seeds of Fascism are within us. Nevertheless, when Fascism has externalized itself in the body of a great power which we have allowed to fatten on our cowardice and crimes, we must actively hate it, better late than never; and help its enemies, whatever their limitations—which perhaps are ours also. Otherwise, spiritually and culturally unprepared, we shall have to fight it alone.

Realizing that the war could draw us in—as it did—he claims that his program *"as a principle of direction . . .* alone could save us." He disclaimed the fears of Aldous Huxley and others that a war against fascism, even if won, would make us become fascized; yet he saw the danger that it could happen. As time went on, this danger—the fascist within us—came to be of even deeper concern to him. And even though fifteen years later we have neither become a fascist state nor moved toward becoming a people joined in a sense of the Cosmos, *Chart for Rough Water* remains valid; the decision has merely been postponed.

Early in 1940 Frank began severing his outside connections to devote himself to research for a novel about New York. But the tumult of problems and disappointments drove him into a depression comparable to those that preceded and followed the time of the lyric novels. He had two strands to cling to; as he put it on page 94 of Notebook XIV, "Two imperative books." One was the novel about the New York of his father, which we shall discuss in due course; the other, a book on the Person, which is only now ready for the press. Both of these, obviously, required much preparation. Both previous periods, similar to the one he was then undergoing, had come to an end in the writing of a novel; one of them, indeed, largely *through* the writing of a novel that projected, on an exaggerated scale, the course he ought not to take. And as with that one, *Chalk Face*, the idea for the new novel came to him suddenly and the book was written quickly. On page 106 of Notebook XIV he plotted the "Theme of Dagny," and two pages later outlined its parts.

Notable in Waldo Frank's writing is an absence of narrative about war. True, he was not ever a soldier; but the same lack has not deterred other writers who wrote in times much less permeated with war than the era of Waldo Frank. That war is the true spur to this novel tentatively entitled "Dagny" is indicated on page 110 of the same notebook: "I am recovering from a reeling, temporary derangement whose immediate cause was indubitably the blitzkrieg in Holland, Belgium, France." He then examines events in his personal affairs that were influenced by this military defeat. And it was in personal terms that he expressed it, just, as we shall later see, the idea of atomic war is expressed in terms of the person in *The Invaders*.

Illness intervened between the events and the writing, begun early in July, of the new novel. And as regularly occurs in Frank's notebooks, when he finally began on the job, cheer replaced gloom. The first draft was completed on September 25, and the title *Summer Never Ends* was finally chosen. Three months later he completed the revision, and when the novel was sent to the publisher, it evoked the same response as did *Chalk Face* eighteen years before; Frank was told that the novel was below his level and would "hurt" him. This time, he changed publishers, and *Summer Never Ends* was brought out by Duell, Sloan and Pearce in 1941.

Summer Never Ends is superficially concerned with an interesting psychological problem: the middle-aged man who falls in love with a woman young enough to be his daughter. Mortimer Crane, a successful corporation lawyer, on the day of the final dissolution of his marriage and estrangement from his wife and children, is interviewed on his abandoned career as a labor lawyer by Dagny Petersen, a graduate student less than half his age, and he is attracted to her. Their affair sets off a number of events in the lives of each of them and the people around them. Mortimer is driven by something apparently akin to an incestuous desire for his daughter, and makes pretty much of a fool of him-

self in pursuing Dagny. He settles too much money on his wife
and separates himself from his children, endowing them with
funds as if he had died and they were receiving their inheri-
tances. He is undiplomatic in his business relationships and
tries to turn back to his idealistic past. He is repelled by his
wife's interest in marrying a man older than she, but refuses to
notice the analogy in his own love affair. He takes advantage of
the respect Dagny gives him on account of his age and position, and at the same time is an aggressive lover.

Dagny is attracted by Mortimer's wealth and fame, and flat-
tered that he should feel a need for her; but she is more attracted by feeling sorry for her fiancé, Herbert Stein, a Jewish
law graduate without a job, who is supported grudgingly by his
sister. Dagny's mother works at a delicatessen in Yorkville,
where they live; her father is an idle carpenter and active Bund-
ist; and her brother is a passive copy of her father. In her life
and her mother's, men are inferior creatures dependent on their
women, and although she is tempted by the comforts Mortimer
Crane could give her, her real sympathies are maternally turned
toward Herbert, who is weak and impotently idealistic. She can
be passionate toward Crane, and this she fights; she cannot be
aroused by Herbert, although she tries very hard to be.

Finally the vitality of Crane inflames her into having intercourse with him. When Herbert learns of it, his jealousy leads
him to tell Dagny's father and to say that Crane is a Jew, so
that Petersen gets a pistol from the Bund arsenal and goes to
Crane's office to shoot him. In dissuading him, Crane debases
himself by revealing that Herbert is really the Jew and by making Petersen his advocate for Dagny. Herbert, his remorse over
using Nazism as a weapon having revealed to him his tragic
weakness, jumps from the Brooklyn Bridge; at the same time
Dagny again visits Crane and reveals her contempt for him by
having intercourse with him again and showing that it does not
affect her. Thus Dagny settles back into the comfort of being

self-sufficient, unaware of Herbert's death but obviously to follow the same path whether he is alive or dead. Crane, now able
to see his place in life clearly, turns back to his children.

It is not an attractive story, but the emotional situation which
it describes—an older man's infatuation for a girl—is common
enough, and the psychological explanation which is in the story
—that the attraction is one of a substitute for incest—seems
penetrating. If Waldo Frank ever experienced this kind of emotion, his astuteness in analyzing it shows astonishing detachment. But to consider this novel merely as a vicarious settling
of an emotional problem of an individual nature is to overlook
both the symbolism in the book and the most significant materials from which the book was made. Waldo Frank, we have
seen, builds his universe from the person. In so doing, he sees
his universe through the person and reflects society in his novels
through the characters in them. "Jews massacred in concentration camps" is the kind of abstraction Frank finds no use for,
any more than he does for "Hitler invades Belgium." "Jews"
means nothing; the word "Jew" can refer to a society, which in
this case is an idea, or to persons. "Hitler" in the second sentence means the German *Macht* in a particular context—most
deeply, the idea of Nazism. Thus these two sentences, which
tortured Waldo Frank, when translated by his method become
persons and ideas. On one level, the Petersens are the idea we
call Nazism—Oskar Petersen obviously the Nazi, stupid and
brutal, authoritarian man; Mrs. Petersen the *Küche, Kirche,
Kinder* woman, his complement; Dagny an incipient Nazism in
America, represented also by the brittle women Crane sees in
New York and Washington. The potentiality of Nazism in his
son and daughter is demonstrated by the ne'er-do-well son of
his old friend, Judith.

The multiplicity of levels becomes evident when we consider
Mortimer Crane and Herbert Stein. Both are projections from
Waldo Frank. The philosophy which renders Herbert ineffectual

is quite reminiscent of the philosophy Frank explicates in *The Re-Discovery of America* and applies in *Chart for Rough Water*. Herbert is the Frank philosophy confronted with force, and lacking a method for handling force. Herbert, in addition, cringes before force, and there is his failure; he lacks confidence in himself. He is a warning to Waldo Frank, the idea, from Waldo Frank, the person. Mortimer Crane, on the other hand, is a warning to Waldo Frank, the person, from Waldo Frank, the idea. Mortimer's danger is alienation. He is strong enough, capable enough of transforming idea into action, but his action may go off in the wrong direction, independent of the things it ought to be a part of. On the level on which Oskar Petersen is the Nazi, Herbert is the Jew, and Mortimer is the well-meaning American.

The characters in *Summer Never Ends* are, in their actions, reminiscent of things in Frank's earlier novels. Dagny, like Quincy Burt, becomes a part of the stream. And Herbert is a somewhat more unwanted Quincy, committing suicide. As David Markand turned to Mary, so Mortimer turns to his children. The climax in Mortimer's life, his decision not to shoot himself with the pistol left by Oskar Petersen, comes from his memory of his mother's love; it is love that will put meaning in life, and after chasing a false love in Dagny, he turns to his children for love. Love, too, is the ingredient of hope at the end of *The Bridegroom Cometh*.

The flaws in *Summer Never Ends* can be also revealed by comparison with earlier work. Like *Chalk Face*, what the book is really about is obscured by what it seems to be about. In fact, the schism is even greater in *Summer Never Ends* because the story itself has too great power. The novels are too easily classified, and Waldo Frank's sense of irony abets the classifiers when he calls *Chalk Face* a mystery story in its dedication and when he subtitled *Summer Never Ends* "A Modern Love Story." In the same way, the structure of *Summer Never Ends* is misleading. On cursory examination it seems to be very conventional in structure. Flashbacks are few, there are no lyric passages, although some verge on the lyric in describing Herbert's moods; the story is told in "movie shot" narrative, with each scene acted out, then followed by another that contributes to a consecutive series, making the tale in just the same way that consecutive scenes are put together in a motion picture. The plan fits the exterior action, but it is out of scale for the deeper symbolism.

Summer Never Ends, in other words, is a novel with a theme that is large enough to be treated on the scale of the symphonic novel, presented in a text only a little larger than that of the lyrics. The chief difference, we must remember, between the lyric novels and the symphonic novels is that the lyrics treated the person, the symphonics both the person and society. The "new lyric" that Waldo Frank was already moving toward would treat the person in society with an intensity emphasizing that salvation for both person and society lies in the person. Using a method condensed from the symphonic, as he did in Summer Never Ends, Frank did not succeed. But nevertheless he was not through with the symphonic method—there remained the novel about New York that he had long wanted to write.

14

Return to America Hispana

AS FAR BACK AS 1910, WALDO FRANK PLANNED TO WRITE A BOOK about Jewish life in New York. In Notebook IV, page 103, he gives it the tentative title "The Godless Ghetto," and indicates that his purpose is to show "that wealthy New York Jews live in as narrow & self-constituting a ghetto as the mediaevals—but save their noble reason of God and a separate mission." That was the idea of a young man rebelling against the society in which he grew up. After he had developed an awareness of the depth of Jewishness in himself—after, in other words, he saw the dynamic quality of Judaism, its roots balancing him in reaching on to the future, Waldo Frank planned books in both directions: a novel, Sabbatai Zevi, that looked back; and The Jewish Word. In time he considered that these might be made into the same book.

On August 7, 1926, he wrote on page 42 of Notebook IX:

Here are the works that I would live to achieve:
    I   David Markand: An American History
    II Aesthetic: the Problem of Value in the Modern World—
to be called
       "The Modern Alchemy" [eventually, The Re-Discovery of America]

III   The Jew and the New World

IV   Toward the American Culture: The Tragic Need of Pan-America to cut free of the Mother-Europe which is dying, and to create its own soul. [Although part was combined with "The Modern Alchemy," this eventually became *America Hispana*.]

By 1934, the Jewish book had again been envisioned as a novel. At the end of the year, on page 12 of Notebook XII, among his "Books Immediately Ahead," Frank listed two volumes of Markand (including the one not written to this day), "Novel on the New York of my Father," a book on Communism, and the book on the Person that was not begun until 1953. After *The Bridegroom Cometh*, Frank began working on plays, and then world affairs, as we have seen, drew him to the writing of *Chart for Rough Water*. Before he wrote *Chart*, however, he had clarified his plans. The goal that still was off in the distance, he indicated on November 12, 1939, was the third and final Markand novel—"But to win the power to approach and achieve that work, I must again learn to live—hearty, deep, and purely. And in the way of this, there are the immediate 'tasks.' 1. World Crisis and America's Future [*Chart for Rough Water*]. 2. The Island in the Atlantic (My New York Saga)."

After the completion of *Chart*, he wrote "Already, there are stirrings in me of the novel *The Island in the Atlantic*." But, as we have seen, *Summer Never Ends* intervened, as an outlet to the conflicts brought on by the tragedy of Hitler's success in Europe. Interruptions continued. Much research had to be done in preparation for writing. Early in 1941 Frank outlined a timetable for the novel, allowing for two interruptions for lecture tours, and planning for publication in the winter of 1944. In view of his plans, and influenced by some question of its strategy, he refused an invitation to tour South America again, and revised his timetable for publication in the autumn of 1943. He had qualms, however, about not accepting the South American invitation, and although he continued his preparation and began writing his novel in July, 1941, he still wanted to express his feeling for the Spanish-speaking peoples, and prepared a revised version of Virgin Spain. After Pearl Harbor the call from South America overpowered that of the novel.

Waldo Frank's tour of South America in 1942 was to some extent a government mission, indirectly sponsored by the State Department for the purpose of counterbalancing the pro-axis influences then at work. It lasted from April to October, and was a refreshing and invigorating experience for him, and his efforts were effective. Indeed, after his tour of Argentina, while he was resting in his apartment in Buenos Aires prior to going on to Chile, he was attacked by a gang of toughs who had obviously come to kill him. By making as much noise as he could, a device he had learned from his companion of the Harlan County experience, he succeeded in scaring them off. Again pictures of the bandage-swathed head of Waldo Frank were featured in the press, and the publicity heightened the effect of his tour. As well as making him more effective, it stirred the fascists to frantic action. The movements of Waldo Frank in South America are headline news down there, but even there it is quite unusual for a creative artist on a lecture tour to be castigated in leaflets distributed through the streets (by employees paid at the back door of the German Consulate), while painted on the walls in large letters was "Muera el Judío Frank!"

The attack put him more in the public eye in the United States as well. Interviews, radio talks, and a series of articles in Collier's magazine made a flurry of interest that he became anxious to exploit. His lectures had been collected and sent to the publisher before his departure from South America, and were issued with the title Ustedes y Nosotros: Nuevo Mensaje á Ibero-América. From the first of November to the middle of January, 1943, he worked on turning the notebook of the journey into a book, and sent it immediately to the printer. South American Journey was published May 20.

South American Journey might have been any one of three very interesting books: it might have been a cultural study of Brazil, which Frank really discovered for the first time after he had written *America Hispana;* it might have been the personal narrative of a journey, like *Dawn in Russia;* or it might have been the account of an antifascist's efforts to offset the influence of Nazi propaganda—the personal history of a campaign that succeeded. Instead it tried to be all three, and although none of the three is inadequately treated, the book lacks focus, like a three-dimensional film on a standard screen. The sections on Brazil are, however, almost of the stature of *Virgin Spain,* tracing the Brazilian heritage from Africa and Portugal and beautifully capturing both the Brazilian sense of destiny and the atmosphere of the land. The anecdotal account of the journey is as charming and full of good humor as *Dawn In Russia.* And the decisive point in the campaign, the attack on Frank in his Buenos Aires apartment, is dramatic and in many ways symbolic both of the whole of the campaign and the whole of World War II. It easily could still be made into the kind of war novel *Summer Never Ends* failed to be.

While *South American Journey* was at the printer's, Frank made a long lecture tour, and when it was completed he prepared again to work on the novel about New York. Feeling unready to begin where he had left off more than a year before, he wrote articles and smaller pieces, and reviewing some of his past work, he discovered that he had written what could almost be a series on Jewish problems; thus was reborn the idea of the book on the Jew. He went to Reno, and while waiting out the divorce decree that concluded his long separation from his second wife, he prepared *The Jew in Our Day* for the press, revived some children's stories he had invented many years before for his son Thomas and had also told to his daughters, with the intention of publishing them some day, and considered writing a book based on the life of the Biblical Jacob. After Reno,

Frank moved on to San Francisco, where he married Jean Klempner. In October he left his Jewish book and his new wife to set out on another lecture tour, rejoining her in New York. Early in 1944 *The Jew in Our Day* was finished.

Made up as it was of articles written as far back as 1925, *The Jew in Our Day* might not have been of the importance it was in molding Waldo Frank's next novel had it not been for the urgency that led him to organize his previous writings on the Jew into a book and write a conclusion for it. Germany, early in 1944, was being defeated, but anti-Semitism was a problem in the United States. Frank identified the traditional Jewish values with those of the Great Tradition of the United States; he had done so for years. But in pointing out wherein Jews are different, and in claiming that their adaptation to the superficial values of the United States is a betrayal of the great tradition of the Jews and of America, he suggested a turning back, a new departure, from these values, this time in the direction of the deeper destiny that he envisions for America, rather than in the direction of imitation of the surface features of American life.

The idea of turning back to go forward, like the idea expressed in *The Jew in Our Day* that Jews' separateness "will again be their bond with all the world," crystallized his concept of the new novel. As soon as *The Jew in Our Day* had been sent to the printer, Frank and his wife retired to Truro, and again he began on *Island in the Atlantic*. This time the materials were ready and no interruptions came. The first draft was completed in about a year, and in 1946 it was published.

15

Island in the Atlantic

THE THIRD STEP IN THE DEVELOPMENT OF WALDO FRANK AND his art was in process. In the lyric novels the relationship between the person and the cosmos is made clear, but since society was not treated, no Person could be shown in action in society. In the symphonic novels, both the person and society are treated but not made one, although the link between them is made strong in *The Bridegroom Cometh*. We see more of the potentiality than of the acts of Markand and Mary. Now was the third step: to unify person, society, and cosmos; to reveal God within the person and God within the society in a way that reveals also the unity of God. The process attempted in *Summer Never Ends* did not succeed in so doing, although the concept was present in embryo. Only some of the themes were sufficiently developed, and the small scale of the book and overemphasis on the theme of the Nazi prevented the other forces in society from coming into focus. It was necessary for Waldo Frank to find some way to present the Person as an operative force in his society.

Already he had been nearly as long in transition from the symphonic novels as he had from the lyric to the symphonic. His interim activity, it is true, was not so exploratory as *The Rediscovery of America*, *Virgin Spain*, and *America Hispana*, but it was as significant to this transition as these works were to the earlier. *Chart for Rough Water* was application of the ideas of

180

Re-Discovery to a particular situation; and the South American lectures made a similar application to the relationship between the Americas.

The direction was already clear, and was more clearly pointed out by *The Jew in Our Day*. Before he wrote that book, and before he had made his lecture tour of South America, he had written about fifty thousand words of the novel about the New York of his father. When he returned to it, almost at a new beginning of his life, happily married and on the way to becoming domesticated for almost the first time in his life, he saw that what he had written was too much like the early symphonic novels. When he began again, it was not to write a symphonic on his father's times, but as a going back, a seeking out of roots. "You got to go back," he had said as bit player in *The Bridegroom Cometh*. And in going back, he found a society in which his father was harmonized as a person.

Island in the Atlantic is not a mere fictionalized biography of Waldo Frank's father. The purpose of the book is to show a time when a person and his society could be in harmony; therefore details had to be altered to show the unity of the individualistic and idealistic Jonathan Hartt and New York between the Civil War and the first World War. In creating Jonathan, Waldo Frank seems to have presented his father as he saw him in retrospect: Waldo Frank playing the rôle of Julius Frank. The chronology is somewhat altered to make the life of Jonathan coincide with the era of expansion in America. Thus, although Julius Frank was born in 1852, Jonathan Hartt is made fifteen years old at the time of the New York draft riots. He is fifty years old in March, 1898, shortly after the sinking of the *Maine*, and his birthday party is as festive as Julius Frank's was in 1902. He dies in 1912, with the era, going down in a sinking like that of the *Titanic*, even though Julius Frank lived until 1931. The two men, however, have the same birthday.

Long before, with *The Dark Mother*, Frank had begun experimenting with the treatment of time in fiction. He came, in *Island in the Atlantic*, to complete abandonment of the "linear" treatment of time, the *roman fleuve*. The book is divided into two parts: "Morning," in which Jonathan is bounded by his life and the city's; and "Afternoon," when, no longer struggling to keep pace with the city, Jonathan's consciousness becomes cosmic. The divisions within these parts are centered each on one day or the events leading up to that day. Thus Frank avoids the thinness of an epic covering so long a period of time. Except in the few portions, most of them centering on Jonathan's partner, Evan Cleeve, Evan's daughter, or Jonathan's son Jeff, the story is told through Jonathan's consciousness. Each of the "days" of the book is crucial for Jonathan and for the nation; and each is symbolic of its particular phase in the development of the characters and the society in which they live.

The first such "day," the section entitled "Hope," is July 13, 1863. During one of the riots against the draft, Jonathan is brought together with Evan Cleeve, son of one of the "great men" of the city. The boys are of the same age and have the same attitude of sympathy for the rioters, as unorthodox for the tradesman-class Jonathan as for the upper-class Evan. Later, with the Cleeves' stable boy, they watch troops fire on the rioters. When the skirmish begins, the stable boy runs for safety with the troops, Evan is hurt, and Jonathan gets him to the Hartts' home to be cared for. The events of this day are symbolic of the whole book, and all of the themes are introduced. The Hartts: Joseph, the father, a pious Jew, kept humble in his business because of his strict adherence to his ideas of right and wrong; Sarah, the Mosaic mother; Reuben, the brother who is already a clever and not scrupulous businessman, and who reports at dinner that Tammany is playing ball with the blue-bloods to use the riots for their own ends; Jonathan's other brother, Philip, who is like his father; his sister Lucia, already active in a club dedicated to women's rights. The Cleeves: Gros-

venor Cleeve, Evan's father, lawyer, politician, connoisseur and
gourmet, whom Evan hates for his coldness to Emma Corthuis
Cleeve, the mother, periodically in bed with a headache that is
clearly psychosomatic. The City: Irish killing Negroes as a protest against exploitation by the bosses; the destruction, seen by
Grosvenor Cleeve on his way to the Mayor's meeting (he sees
it in terms of property) at which he will join in the plan to
delay the offer from the Governor of Connecticut of troops
already available, so that the uprising will develop to the point
where any independence in the lower classes can be crushed
along with it; the same destruction seen by the boys in terms of
humanity, as they sympathize both with the Negroes and the
Irish, and stand with the rioters when the troops fire—at the
same time Grosvenor Cleeve is consummating the deal; the miserable and the cracked, crowded together in the warrens of
the city. And finally, Hope: the hope that the riots will help
the oppressed; the hope in the Hartts' maid, Frieda, and her
fiancé, Martin Schmitt, for the farm they plan to own; the hope
that Jonathan sees in having Evan Cleeve as a friend, in living
in the world Grosvenor Cleeve describes as full of opportunity.
This is the hope of Jeffersonian democracy, that individualism
will result in the common good, the hope that died from the
time of the Civil War to the time of the Great War.

The vividness and the variety of the first fifty pages of the
first section are astonishing. The economy is even more remarkable in retrospect, for all the potentialities in the characters and
the era are revealed, as are the obstacles that would permit the
development of only one set of these potentialities. Yet it is
still the story of three boys on a day in 1863, told with verisimilitude that is satisfying without reference to the symbolism
that explores the lives of those boys and their era.

"Mirages," the second section, is broken down into three
days: the day in 1871 when Evan's mother commits suicide
and Evan and Jonathan become law partners; the day in 1877

when Jonathan and Grete Mendis agree to marry, with a prelude of July 4, 1876, when Jonathan's father dies; and the day in 1889 when Jonathan, rather than go against his principles, determines to reveal Evan's dishonest deals with Tammany, tells him, and thereby causes him to leave New York. The title "Mirages" is apt, not just because many of the hopes of the previous section turned out to be mirages, but because as they are revealed as such they suggest that Jonathan's whole rationalist-Jeffersonian dream is a mirage.

The third part counterpoints Evan's life outside of New York with scenes of the childhood and youth of Jonathan's son, Jefferson. This is the only section of the book not centering on a day, and its title, "The Waters Flow Through the Land," symbolizes the indirection of Evan, cast up on the shores of Elysium, a river town, obviously Cincinnati. He takes a room with a Bohemian family, gets a job in the symphony orchestra, and meets a Quaker schoolteacher, Rachel Lorne; he marries Rachel, and makes a failure of his marriage and his work in his drive toward destruction. They have a daughter, Rebecca, who grows up to despise her father as he despised his. Theme and counterpoint are drawn together as Evan wanders back to New York, arriving on the night of Jonathan's fiftieth birthday, only to die in Jonathan's house a few days later.

The second half of the novel, "Afternoon," opens with the passage of time sharply emphasized in the life of Jonathan. The sale of his Upper West Side house, the death of his mother, the return of his son Jeff from studying at the *Beaux Arts* marks the end of a part of his life. Jonathan has a sordid affair with a widow, Mrs. Louella Lake, whom he meets while he is engaged in selling his house. The affair is echoed in Jeff's affair with Rebecca, the daughter of Evan Cleeve, and themes are entwined as in the opening of the book when Rebecca takes up also with Marius Schmitt, the son of the Frieda who was maid with the Hartts' when Jonathan was a child. Marius is a radical, and he and Rebecca go to Paris, while Jonathan is extricated from Mrs. Lake's attempt to blackmail him by his practical brother Reuben. Jeff, however, confesses his affair to his wife, who agrees that he must find her and make an end to one or the other of his loves, and Jonathan decides to accompany him on the quest to Paris.

This section is entitled "Bread Cast Upon the Waters." The last section is entitled "Knowledge," and shows the return on what is heedlessly set in train. Marius, Rebecca, and Jeff go off together to the Ile d'Oléron. When Jonathan, mystically summoned, follows them there, he learns that partly through Jeff's fault, Marius has died. In this situation the nature of Rebecca, completely lost, the destroyer, is revealed, and Jeff is made free to return to America with Jonathan on the maiden voyage of the Cosmopolis.

All the symbolism of the book comes home to roost in the concluding portion, on board the ship. The Island in the Atlantic of the book is, of course, Manhattan, not quite America, partly European. The social milieu of the first half of the book is this Atlantic island on the immigrant's road from Europe to America, the place where many stop, never getting to the mainland. Evan Cleeve, vestige of Europe through his upper-class status, could visit the mainland only to spawn and die. Another island in the Atlantic is the Ile d'Oléron, near Bordeaux, where Jeff, Marius, and Rebecca showed that they, as projections into the twentieth century of their nineteenth century parents and the classes and political attitudes they represent, could not survive.

Still another island in the Atlantic is the ship Cosmopolis. Comfortable in their cabin on C deck, Jonathan and Jeff are aware of the immigrants in the steerage as they were not in their island of Manhattan. Jonathan visits the steerage with an Anglican priest, and they see sights reminiscent of City Block. The other side of the island is represented in Jonathan's dinner at the Captain's table. The diners discuss finance, and one of them incidentally comments, "a boat like this would be better business if she went down."

"So they'd have to build another?" Reuben nodded.

"To keep the credit moving? Banks, insurance companies, shipyards?" Murtry nodded.

Carvies said, "It would be all right if she could go down—without loss of public confidence."

"Or loss of life?" Jonathan smiled.

"Public confidence," Carvies ignored him, "is needed to keep the credit going."

"Yes," said Murtry. "If ships or factories could just disappear without scaring the public and freezing their money—"

"There's a problem for you, Sir Archibald," said Reuben.

"I think I know how it might be done." Jonathan sipped his coffee.

For the first time they really looked at him.

"War," said Jonathan.

They all protest that a war between great powers is impossible. The great powers are too comfortable; would not upset the apple cart. And that night the unsinkable ship strikes an iceberg and sinks. There are not enough lifeboats, and Jonathan sacrifices himself to save his son.

Jonathan thus achieves himself as a Person. Representative of his background of Jeffersonian democracy, he was optimistic all through "Morning," in spite of the flaws obvious to him in his world. In 1870 or so, he and Evan had title searched and got a deed for the land Frieda and Martin Schmitt were squatting on, near the East River. Jonathan took a bottle of wine with him when he delivered the deed, but he found Frieda alone, and after drinking, he had intercourse with her. Although he had picked a time when he thought Martin would be at home, and Frieda did the seducing, he was so remorse-stricken he never went back; thus he never learned that shortly afterward, his brother Reuben swindled the Schmitts out of their land and thereby warped the childhood of young Marius. If his conscience had not prevented him from keeping in touch with them, he could have prevented the downfall of the Schmitts. His principles led him to refuse to let the matter of Evan's dishonesty in deals with Tammany be quashed, although Evan's father hushed it up, and thereby destroyed his friend (who, however, wished to be destroyed), estranged himself with his wife, and lost most of his business. When, at the ebb of his career, he was offered a partnership in a large but not very scrupulous law firm, he twice refused it. By himself, he won a place in his world, and then found it empty. In his worst moment, he turned to Mrs. Lake.

The upswing began with books Jeff brought him as a present from France; particularly with what they had to say about the Jews. Slowly, he abandoned his rationalism, his faith in Jeffersonianism. When he came to know Marius, particularly in Paris, he became aware of how lives are entangled. His mystical experience, knowing, without physical contact, that Jeff is in trouble, is a sign of the growth of that awareness to a sense of the unity of all things. His having enough faith in his extrasensory perception to go to the Ile d'Oléron shows that he has become a Person. His act as a person is sacrificing himself for his son, going down with the nineteenth century to save a potential person into the twentieth.

In similar ways all the themes are developed. Paddy, the stable boy who deserted Jonathan and Evan in the draft riots, symbolizes the working class of 1863, particularly the Irish in New York, who deserted their destiny to Tammany. Philip, a salesman who shifts from job to job yet preserves his ingenuousness, is the mild Jew living at peace with the world but something of a victim. Reuben's besmudged career is traced through business deals and political deals to the ministry to China in the McKinley administration, when the germs of the Chinese repudiation of America were sown. Lucia and Reuben's daughter both become impotent advocates of human rights—Lucia remaining concerned with feminism; Reuben's daughter turning to Zionism. In Evan we have the disintegration of the privileged, the leisure class. Although he is charming and his life contains beauty in his music, he hates his heritage and the cruelty of his father so much that he destroys himself; his daughter carries on only his destructive side. Marius is destroyed as the socialist movement of Europe was destroyed, of its own weakness in the face of the Great War. His end is as tragic as the desertion of Paddy.

In the section on Evan in Elysium, many figures appear who symbolize the diversity and potentiality of mainland America. Evan stays at the boarding house of Mrs. Liebling, the Scotch widow of a Viennese musician, whose cuisine is an amalgam of dishes from the two lands. Her house is full of as exotic a mixture of people: her two sons, Tam, who is the practical manager of the household, and Jacob, tall, golden, and capable of glorious drinking bouts; and the boarders, like Dresden figures:

> As Evan stood at the door, she introduced him name after name to her boarders. Over their heads on the mirrored mantelpiece he saw a row of Dresden figures. He heard: Mrs. Goldberg, Herr Marks, Madame Dolores, Miss Madden, the Count . . . and saw the china shepherdess, the roaring lion, the fiddler, the pierrot; saw them doubled by their reflection in the glass.

The country, the city, the people—these themes develop entwined in the days of *Island in the Atlantic*. Not once is a date mentioned—the time can be traced only by events: and the events come to life like characters. Small factual errors in the book suggest that Frank made the people and setting of a past time in New York vivid by transposing the reference books and the pictures in the museums to his own experience, seeing the New York he knows well, but seeing it in its form of the sixties, seventies, and eighties. For example, Jeff as a young boys walks from his parents' house on the West Side to visit his grand-mother near Park Avenue. He walks past the house to watch the puffs of smoke from a locomotive coming through the grat-ings in the New York Central tunnel under the avenue. "He watched the smoke leap upward, block by block. Now it was where he stood, now it was rolling away . . . uptown . . . farther away: the wonderful train. It would come out of the ground at One-hundred-twenty-fifth Street." No one knows better than Waldo Frank that the New York Central tracks emerge from under Park Avenue just above Ninety-sixth Street; he was de-scribing his own experience watching the locomotives on the New York Central freight line, by Riverside Park, where he played as a child. There they emerge at One hundred twenty-fifth Street. As a child he had seen the puffs of smoke coming from the gratings on Park Avenue, but he was more familiar with them on the West Side, and the images blended in his mind.

Although old New York is convincingly recreated, *Island in the Atlantic* is not like a historical novel in exploiting the pic-turesqueness of the past; its seeking out of roots and causes is deeper, a thing of psychological and social forces as well as Frank's vision of the person and society. For instance, unlike the Marxists, who for the most part consider the tendency toward collectivism in American history a development solely toward economic equality, he is aware that corporations are just as much collectives as cooperatives are. The political Jeffersonianism that fails in the book is the notion that the greatest individualism will produce the greatest collective good. When talking to an advocate for big business, to which he objects, Jonathan is told not to talk like a socialist, and he replies, "I'm no Socialist, Sam. I believe in our system of private enterprise and in the Consti-tution. Maybe your railroads are the Socialists and don't know it." When the radical socialist fails because the violence he ad-

vocates is used against him, it becomes clear that Frank has gone
to the roots of the collectivism-individualism duality, found
them one, and found them rotten.

There is confusion between Jonathan and Jeff, not as characters, but as themes. Waldo Frank plays both rôles, and as Jeff
he plays himself born when his brother was and undergoing a
development he did not undergo. The growth to awareness that
Jonathan achieves, on the other hand, was achieved by Waldo
Frank at a much earlier age than Jonathan's; then when Jeff is
set on the path of the same growth, there is nothing more to
say. Father and son are both symbols of the person; Jonathan
that of the age of expansion, Jeff of the present. We see nothing of Jeff's development beyond Jonathan's death; thus *Island
in the Atlantic* is only a step toward treatment of the Person
in the society of today, even though it is successful with yesterday.

The development of Jonathan into a whole Person had to be
accompanied by his death, for his achievement of himself was
only possible in the era that ended with the coming of the Great
War. He did not just sacrifice himself by going down with the
ship; he was completed at that point. His spiritual self might
have remained intact no matter how much longer he lived, but
his sociology would not. He would not be equal to the world he
lived in any more than his brother Philip, the projection of his
father, was equal to Jonathan's world. Joseph, Jonathan's father,
and Philip were persons of an Old Testament world; Jonathan
was a person of a Jeffersonian, rational world, although he came
to recognize its flaws; for the world after the Great War, a new
kind of person would be needed. And it was in preparation for
creating in fiction that kind of person that Waldo Frank wrote
first about the previous kind.

The evocation of America, however, is more nearly universal.
The perfectly achieved characterization is New York City. Like
the other characters, the city grows, not just physically, but as

personality. The group conversations in restaurants and at the Radical Club, the parties, the meetings, all join with the physical expansion in presenting a picture of the city in growth, a living thing. Somehow, without losing the realism and sweep of the symphonic novel, *Island in the Atlantic* has in it the poetic quality of *City Block.* I suspect that limiting each section to one day in one consciousness, and increasing scope only by associations made by events of that one day in that one consciousness, helped make each section lyric. The only section that varies from that method to give a sweep of time is that of Evan in Elysium, and there the symbolism creates the illusion of a moment in time. Evan is, after all, not in Cincinnati, but in Elysium, which is both the mainland of America and at the same time Limbo. Although it is populated with the people of America, for Evan it is Limbo, and from the time he leaves Jonathan's office to escape prosecution until he comes to Jonathan's house to die, is but a moment in his career. Nothing has been changed in him, but merely carried to its logical conclusion.

Most remarkable of all in *Island in the Atlantic* is its completeness. Jonathan, the city, the era, grow up and are transfigured. The effect of 1863-1912 on New York City is easy to see; seeing it, we should be able to see how this era of expansion created today; and focusing clearly on the person of that era gave Waldo Frank the power to create as literary character the person of today.

16

The Invaders

THERE SEEMS TO BE A PATTERN EVEN TO WALDO FRANK'S "SEMI-nal periods," the times between books. When he is moving toward a work of cultural criticism, he writes political articles, is something of a pamphleteer; and when he has in process a further development in his fiction, he writes plays. Although his next "essential book" was the planned work on the Person, he knew he was not ready to write it. Without knowing what was to come next, he automatically began planning a play.

Between the writing of *Island in the Atlantic* and the time it was published, World War II came to a close with the use of the atomic bomb, and relief at the end of the fighting was soon superseded by fear of the weapon we used being used against us. Waldo Frank had long felt that selfish nationalism is as destructive of the nation as blind individualism is of the person; the use of atomic weapons served, however, as a device for dramatizing that possible destruction. His play, therefore, was planned to show the person confronted by the destructiveness of atomic war. The play, however, turned out to be a novel, *The Invaders*.

The novels of Waldo Frank are made from ingredients in his life. He has been at times ruthless with himself, revealing the most secret thoughts of his mind, the most insane potentialities of his personality, the most hidden motives in his acts. It is as if he were two people, the Waldo Frank who is hit over the head in Kentucky or in Argentina, and the Observer, who, without being involved in the action, sees all that occurs, notes it down, and uses it in the making of fiction. His whole life has gone into his writing, from the philosophy fundamental to his outlook to the things he has seen, the people he has known, and the happenings of his experience. These things he blends, both consciously and unconsciously, to create things he has not seen, people who have not lived, and happenings that never occurred.

In *The Invaders*, a novel of almost mid-point transition from the symphonic to the new lyric, the process of creation in Waldo Frank can best be observed. The lyric technique, modified to reveal the consciousness of society as well as that of the person, was used in *Island in the Atlantic*, but since the society of that novel was, in respect to time, past, the lyricism never became personal. In writing of the present, since he must because of the essential purpose behind his work, get inside his characters to the extent that he touches the quick in his readers, Frank becomes so personal that squeamish readers are offended; all readers are shocked. The society described in *Island in the Atlantic* was a completed one, and the symphonic framework on which the lyric sections were placed helped provide perspective and remoteness. Each reader today of Frank's works of the present is a part of the society being described, and the lyric structure emphasizes that he is a participant in the book.

The Invaders tells of an event that did not occur—the dropping on New York City of a new sort of atomic bomb that kills without destroying property. The bomb is dropped "accidentally" from one of our own planes, and it sets off political repercussions that result in nearly the whole world declaring war on the United States, the clamping down of military dictatorship here, and an enemy attack on New York in which a conventional atomic bomb is dropped. The action, except for lyric passages on the bombings, takes place in and around the cottage on the New England coast inhabited by Mark Ferry, a retired architect, his wife Bianca, and their infant, Christopher. Their retirement is invaded, after the first bomb is dropped, by refugees from the city: Mara, Mark's divorced wife, their two teen-age children, Bayard and Beth, and Lew Dachill, Mara's lover. In addition, Clare Locke, a *gueule cassée* of World War II—former Jew, former Communist, former suitor of Bianca's—arrives driven by the end-of-the-world feeling to seek her again. Since the bomb, in real life, was not dropped, this invasion of the cottage obviously did not occur; nor are any of the characters representations of real people. But by taking the potentialities, both of real people and of characters in his earlier novels, Waldo Frank created these people and this situation, created them and the milieu in which they live with a warp that had to be straightened out by cruel and shocking means.

The love that Mara once had for Mark has been turned to hate; because he is happy in his present marriage, she hates Bianca. The effect of this hate on Bayard and Beth is mixed; their attitude to their father is both love and hate, with Beth more sympathetic toward him, distressed only that her parents could not get along together, and Bayard siding with his mother.

The events take place from the evening of the arrival until the following evening. Locke, having arrived later than the rest, is bedded down in the living room. During the night, Beth goes down for a glass of milk, and gives herself to him. He interprets her act to her the next day:

> "It occurs to me," he said, "that all it meant for you was you felt sorry for me. 'Here's a poor war victim, he's given his face for his country; I'll show him a girl can be a hero too. If he offers his beautiful face, I'll offer my beautiful body.' Something like that, wasn't it? And sorry for yourself. 'I'll show 'em! I'll throw away my beautiful body: that'll teach Mom and Pop, who couldn't get along and who hurt me.' . . ."

This act of compensation was Beth's effort to overcome the flaw in the house—hate. Before the invasion, the house was without it; the coming of Mara has brought it in. And Mark is aware that when Mara leaves, the flaw—or the ghost of it— will remain. Bianca thinks only of how things were; she wants to clean these people and what they brought with them out of her house as she would sand blown in on a windy day. Mark, knowing that this cannot be done, wants them to stay until the matter is resolved. He says, ". . . we few people in this house with a white fence around it must learn to help each other live, or there's no hope anywhere." Mara is possessive, selfish, and Mark feels he must respond to her hate with love. "People are hurt," he says, ". . . and in a self-defense hurt others. And these always in self-defense hurt others: the endless bloody circle! With all the inertia of tradition, right, duty and love, to keep it going and to keep us caught! Someone must jump out of it, Bianca!"

The victim is Beth, since she had already elected the position of victim by her act with Locke. Out swimming, she goes too far, and drowns. She might have been saved, except that Bayard and Locke were disputing, and thus they did not watch her. When her body is recovered and brought to the cottage, Mara, like the woman in the *City Block* story, "Murder," in a paroxysm of rage and need, crushes Bianca's infant. Thus the circle continues, but it is modified. Bayard asks to stay with his father, but Mark sends him on, telling him his mother has greater need of him now. Bianca, determined to leave, asks Locke to take her with him, but he refuses. Nevertheless, since her sanctuary has been invaded, she goes, and Mark is left alone. "What he had done to them all must not have been in vain. There was Cause for what he had done; although fleshed in his fumbling and failure, there was Truth, and he must not betray it. . . ."

Counterpoint to the invasion of the cottage is New York

when the bomb is dropped. Simultaneous with Bianca's discovery of Christopher's death is the second bomb in Manhattan.
The link between Mark Ferry confronted with violence and a
nation confronted with violence is clear. The bomb that started
it all was from one of our own planes; it was not by answering
betrayal with love that Mark set in train the events at the
cottage, but as part of his earlier relationship with Mara. Mark
fails, but only because he had been clumsy; his fundamental
method was right, and may still come right. Two hopes remain:
Bayard has turned toward him, and Bianca is pregnant; they will
return to him, because he acted with love in sending them away.
The nation, on the other hand, having brought violence on
itself by means of its own bomb, reacted with violence, and even
if it could defeat the rest of the world in war, would have lost
to the military dictatorship it imposed on itself. A symbolic
unity, created through lyric connections between the bombings
of New York and the events at the cottage, makes one the
person and society; and the solution Frank would offer is inherent in that unity.

Anyone who has read both *Summer Never Ends* and *The Invaders* would notice a strong similarity between Mark Ferry and
Mortimer Crane; between Mara Ferry and Leila Crane; and
between Lew Dachill and MacDonald Stotes. The children of
the stories are both a boy and a girl; the boy more distant at first,
but coming to a greater understanding of his father. Clare Locke,
however, and Bianca, are new. Even the similar characters, of
course, are modified. Mark is Mortimer, modified by Jeff Hartt,
of *Island in the Atlantic*, and married to a woman who seems
exactly what he needs as a wife. He loses her, not because his
attempt to stop the circle of hate was inharmonious with her
character, but because he failed to stop it in time. Mara is
Leila modified by Rebecca, of *Island*. Dachill is a younger Stotes,
not a lawyer, but a more vicious parasite on the money-men—
a public relations counsel, spy, and stool-pigeon. The events

evolve from the characters, as, in Frank's philosophy, events naturally evolve from persons, or at least are at one with them. Thus it comes clear that Frank created his story from modifying and projecting combinations of his former characters, probably themselves projected from the potentialities in actual people, and added new characters, largely as catalysts, who were probably also projected from the potentialities of real people. The two new major characters, Locke and Bianca, apparently projections of real people, unmodified by previous existence in the fiction of Waldo Frank, are more obviously symbols, less capable of independent action. Frank is wise to make such characters catalysts rather than fully active ingredients; it is only after a character of his has had some kind of fictional experience with Frank himself that the fullest depth of character-portrayal in Frank's power is achieved. The lesser characters, the neighbor woman, the handyman Tom-Jeff, and Isaac Mather and Daniel Dunne, the authoritarian and libertarian selectmen, are drawn directly from real people, as Frank's lesser characters always are. The setting also is real: it is Cape Cod.

Clear evidence of the development and integration of Frank's art is that in this book, where we can for the first time since the early lyrics distinguish by outside evidence the three layers of projections—the projections from earlier projections, the projections from people, and the projections of people—no disruption of verisimilitude exists. Mark and Mara are as real-sounding people as Tom-Jeff and the neighbor woman. Some crochets exist in the lesser characters; they are, like Dickens's characters, a trifle too picturesque—and for the same reason, since they too are caricatures done from life. Their talk, like the talk of the characters in an E. A. Robinson poem, is too typically New England talk. "Isaac Mather scarce moved his lips to say: 'Tell Mrs. Ferry the roof shud hold for a spell now. But I don't guarantee. The hull south side needs reshinglin'.' " "So I was out for a walk. With the sun still burning a hole in the west, you could see a star in the east. I had a funny idea it looked like a cinder. The star. . . . Now, I asked myself, what if the wind blows that cinder of a star into the sun's eye. The sun wouldn't go out, but it certainly would blink like the very devil. It would get still colder. It's damn cold for October," says Roberta, the neighbor woman.

For the modern reader, the handling of some of the comments of the voice from the radio does, however, disturb the illusion. Following a tradition that has been out of fashion of late, Frank rarely mentions the actual name of a commodity, but alters it. In *Island*, writing about an earlier time, he used such names as "Sapolio" and some others that probably also are the names of products no longer manufactured, but he does not use the names of current products in *The Invaders*. Thus when he emphasizes the irony of business as usual in a world headed for destruction by the device of reproducing the commercials along with the news broadcasts about the bombing of New York, and even re-writes singing commercials, he merely emphasizes that he cannot turn his talents to slick publicizing of commercial products. He is impatient with the details of popular radio production to the extent that he calls the station XYZ, when it would have been just as easy to have invented call letters that sound real, and merges a commercial into a news report, even though that is contrary to present broadcasting procedure. These things, however disturbing they may be to the reader of today, will probably not even be noticed after the mannerisms of radio have had a chance to shift. A similar outrage against the reader's technical knowledge, one that might always be a flaw in the book, is the explanation given over the radio of the bomb that could kill without destroying property:

". . . It kills like it was putting to sleep. In an exclusive interview Professor Victor Doppelsicht, once of Berlin University and for years connected with United States Army Research, told me, and I quote: 'A certain element that must not be named, present in

limitless quantities in a certain edible vegetable that must not be
named, but that has a peculiar color and is much used in preparation of a soup called borscht, is known to be fissionable after being
processed by a certain secret method. But the radioactivity, instead
of exploding, silently diffuses the lower atmosphere—' "

A mind that could produce the excellent symbol of the dream
of the predatory forces of a nation, an atomic bomb that would
not destroy property, and then have the bomb made from beets,
shows an impatience with technical details that clashes with conventions, Especially ironical is the blundering usage implying
that radioactivity explodes in a nuclear weapon when we consider
that this prediction of the poisoning of the atmosphere with
radioactivity was made in 1948, and it was not until 1955 that,
in veiled hints from Sir Anthony Eden and the director of the
Los Alamos laboratory, the possibility of a weapon producing
radioactive poisoning without an explosion was announced. I
have no doubt that Frank perpetrated his grotesque joke on
purpose; it is both a literary and a cultural criticism.

No such flaw appears—or clashes—in the lyric passages showing the ramifications of the actions at the cottage: the New
York scenes. In four places—the skyscrapers of downtown, a
penthouse on the Upper East Side, a tenement in the Lower
East Side, and an apartment near Columbia University—we see
certain groups of people, first before the bomb, then during
and after. Mingled in with these are other city scenes, some of
those who escape, some of those who die. The section ends:

> The winds eddied. In all directions they gusted, innumerably,
> as if seeking a leader and assembly. They were . . . the winds . . .
> like the people. On Exchange Place, the handcart of a newsdealer
> lay overturned. Its papers had spilled into the gutter and the chaotic
> winds blew them in all ways: toward Broadway, toward Broad
> Street, up to Wall Street. Pages of the papers scattered and spread:
> pictures of pugilists, politicians, aviators, dancers; advertisements of
> funeral parlors, baby foods, television, the new plastic wonder-

girdle; accounts of the Stock Market, of the United Nations, of the city scandal, blew with the comics and the president's address. Against a draingate below the Sub-Treasury porch, a page flattened: the statue of George Washington looked down on Superman soaring toward the sun to rescue a maiden, and on a photograph of starving Hindus in Calcutta.

For the reader who is in too big a hurry to reflect on this symbolism of the father of his country looking at his country's dreams and the results of its actuality, *The Invaders* contains many things not immediately clear. When, after the body of Beth has been brought from the sea, and Mara left upstairs with her, Bianca goes up to look at the baby asleep in his room, the people in the room below hear a shriek—and the scene shifts to Times Square. Jack Oray, a former sailor, observes the commercial hodgepodge, is jostled by the crowds, but notices he hears nothing.

—I can't *hear* nothing! Jack Oray was puzzled. He had seen the work of plenty of bomb explosions. He remembered that when he heard them, they were at a distance. Was he *in* this one? was that why he heard nothing? All the stuff he saw, the gadgets and the billboards and the buildings and the surging people, could have got mixed up, only because the explosion was now!

He touched his chest: solid, not a scratch. Then, he heard. He heard the city. He heard the shriek of the city. . . .

And the shriek of Bianca is picked up in the next section, her shriek at finding her infant dead, in Mara's arms. This is the only indication that a second bomb has fallen on New York —and it is ambiguous. If a bomb did not fall, it is as if a bomb had fallen; that is enough. But the subtlety of the passage would be beyond many readers, who might think it mere decoration, or out of place. Not only is the reader expected to be very perceptive, but he is expected to know some words that are not commonly used in fiction. Frank has always displayed a very large vocabulary, but in this novel he seems occasionally to use words wilfully to confuse the imperfect reader. In the lyric passage of the first bomb, the spotlight falls for a moment on a subway train and its already crowded passengers; then Frank adds, in parenthesis, "in forty-five minutes the cars would be inspissated to a solid mass." From the context, knowing that a bomb was to be dropped on New York, the reader who does not know the word *inspissated* would deduce that they were blown up or melted by the heat of an explosion, and would miss for some pages the point that the bomb did not produce a blast, but a contamination. The word means *thicken*; the parenthetical remark merely refers to the packed-solid condition of the rush hour subway trains—and the subway passengers spotlighted for a moment escaped safely to Queens. The impact of one of the most important symbols in the novel is jeopardized by one wilfully-chosen word.

The bitterness in Waldo Frank which such ambiguities reveal was not to last long. *The Invaders* is a very personal novel. It would almost seem that to use the setting of one's home for a novel of this sort would be to make the house haunted with the events and characters, and such may have been the case by the time the book was finished. In addition, although *Island in the Atlantic* had quite good reviews and a fair success in sales in this country, Waldo Frank felt that he was being forgotten without ever having been understood. That bitterness is only occasional in *The Invaders* is quite astonishing in view of these facts. But a call from Latin America prevented his bitterness from growing.

17
Not Heaven

ALTHOUGH THE EARLY NOTEBOOKS ABOUND WITH SHORT STORY themes, between 1922 and 1947 Waldo Frank wrote only two stories, both of which were published in *Esquire* magazine, and one of which was awarded a place in the O'Brien *Best Short Stories of 1935*. In the twenties, Frank had started a special notebook for short story themes, transferring to it all that he had already noted in the general notebooks, and making any further entries for stories directly in it. When he finished *The Invaders* in 1947, he decided to revive some of his short story ideas and had written several when, in 1948, he was invited to attend the inauguration of Rómulo Gallegos, the Venezuelan novelist, as president of Venezuela. He accepted, conscious of the honor in being considered a sort of godfather to the liberal administration coming into office. During the festivities, that centered more on cultural and artistic activities than one would expect of a political affair, talk naturally turned to the career of Simon Bolívar, and Frank was asked if he would write a life of the South American liberator. In *America Hispana* Frank had written of Bolívar, "He was a romantic poet."

> Bolívar felt the pregnancy of the American world . . . the Indian, the Negro, the mestizo, the Forest and the Mountain were, for him, the elements of a tragic parturition. He envisaged the emergence, from this continental plasm, of a new race. And when he said that he would rather be Liberator than Caesar, he meant that he would

free these turbulent potencies, deliver them to themselves, in order that they might come at last to birth.

The Venezuelans knew that Frank's vision of America was in harmony with Bolívar's. Thus the new government not only felt that Frank was the ideal interpreter of Bolívar's life, but they offered to subsidize the writing of the book. In short, the proposition was made so attractive, and Frank was so much in sympathy with the idea, that he agreed. He worked for three years, immersing himself in the world of Bolívar, both through documents and by visiting the scenes of Bolívar's life. Before the end of 1948, the constitutional government was overthrown by revolt, but the new government, in spite of Frank's opposition to them, honored the agreement—an indication of the unusual and deep kinship Latin America has for Waldo Frank. *The Birth of a World* was published in the United States and England as Frank wrote it, was soon translated into French, but the Venezuelan government, controlling some of the rights in Spanish, delayed the issuance of a Spanish translation for some years.

The book is more than a biography. In it Frank achieved, on the level of history, the objective he had been working toward in his fiction—the organic synthesis of a people and a person. The subject of the biography was ideal for this purpose. Bolívar emerged from his people, undergoing a trial of chaos within himself like that South America is still undergoing. From his greatest adversities he created his most effective campaigns, his vision of an America to be, and himself as a Person. The life of Bolívar can be made a symbol of the development he dreamed of in his people, and his finding a mystical rebirth at the moment of greatest adversity makes him like the protagonist of a Waldo Frank novel. In recognition of the symbolic development of a people in a person, *Birth of a World* is unique.

Just as exposition of the vision expressed in the lyric novels

and later in the symphonic novels had provided Waldo Frank
with firm platforms on which to build further, so the exemplifica-
tion of the unity of a person and a people in the past, first
expressed in *Island in the Atlantic*, became possible through
Birth of a World. The Bolívar book, although the biography of
a nineteenth century person, is a study of the Latin America
of past, present, and future. Waldo Frank returned to his short
stories.

With the example of *City Block* before him, it is difficult to
say just when Waldo Frank realized that the stories he had
chosen to write were ingredients for a story cycle. Quite probably
the idea was in his mind, at least subconsciously, when he chose
which themes to develop into stories. The form of the cycle was
one which can be seen evolving in *The Invaders*, in the death of
Beth, who felt that she had reached a dead end, and so swam
until she could no longer reach shore. *Not Heaven* was completed late in 1952, and was published in April, 1953.

It is astonishing just how far back the *Not Heaven* stories go,
although none of them was written until after *The Invaders*.
The earliest theme was noted down on page 11 of Notebook
VII, and since it was suggested by the suicide of the Cromwell
twins, American Red Cross girls who leaped together from the
ship carrying them home from France in February, 1919, it was
probably put down while the story was still in the newspapers.
It eventually became the story "Culture of the West." On page
93 of the same notebook is the original of "Samson." Page 105
has the germ of "Victory." The long Prelude, "Antient History,"
was suggested by a theme for a novel on pages 88-9 of Notebook
VIII, probably recorded early in 1925. "The Cat," with a point
similar to that of the final version, was recorded later in the
same year. The fantasy mid-piece of the book, "The Red Sea,"
is recorded under the same title two pages later, on page 14 of
Notebook IX, and back on page 123, late in 1928, was noted
the subject for "The Last Word." The theme story itself, "The

Kingdom of Heaven," was probably recorded early in 1929, for it appears on page 5 of Notebook X. The remaining six cannot be dated, for they were recorded directly into the story note-book. The reason for seeking out these first stirrings of the book, however, is to show that they are drawn from a vast number of story themes accumulated over thirty years, and that some of them were considerably altered to fit the overall purpose. "Victory," for example, began as a mere ironic incident. The note reads:

Tale

The man who overcomes his attraction for his daughter by thrusting her into the arms of another man . . . his crony . . . a brute like himself.

In its final form, this is merely an incident in the story. Joe Pulsa, tempted by his daughter's beauty, brings home a French Canadian "devil with the women" to live with them. The crony runs away, leaving the girl pregnant and with gonorrhea, and after a miscarriage, she goes blind. In spite of her blindness, she brightens her father's life with her beauty and the music she turns to. When a young composer wants to marry her, Joe hap-pily agrees, although his life will be empty without her, and after her departure, he merely stops taking care of himself. Finally sure that she will no longer need him, when she sends clippings of her success as a musician, he dies.

They put him in a pine box, which the carpenter threw together from old boards in the barn, and five men carried it up the hill and down to the hollow where they had dug a grave. As they went up, the box—heavy enough when they first lifted it (Joe was a stocky, muscled man), grew lighter. At the crest of the hill, suddenly it tried to soar, and the hands of the five, gripping hard, had to hold it down. Over the crest, as they descended, the soaring passed, but the coffin was light, as if empty. Three of the five men were old farmers, neighbors of Joe Pulsa; one worked in the town garage; the fifth was the carpenter. Not one mentioned what had happened to him—not to the others, not to a soul. Most folk talk, even to wife or husband, only of what they judge will be judged sane. So the miracle was never spoken, and unshared became unreal. . . .

In a "Note to the Reader" after the last story, Frank cites precedents in arguing why he considers his short story cycle a novel, and points out in so doing that both the unifying quality and the difference between his collection and preceding ones evolves from his concept of the person. In *City Block* he had merely noted, on the page facing the table of contents, "*The author assures the reader that* City Block *is a single organism and that its parts should be read in order.* . . ." It should be enough for a writer to say: What I have written has an overall plan; if you consider only its parts in isolation from each other, you are missing part of what the book has to offer. The whole is more than the sum of its parts. It is because *Not Heaven* has no characters, setting, or other physical unifier in common among the stories, and because the stories are more satisfying as entities than the *City Block* stories that Waldo Frank felt the need to explain his intention. As a novel, *Not Heaven* is about Heaven and Hell; how to get to Heaven and what Hell is like. It is based on an idea that is like a combination of the three quotations at the front of the book:

WHEN ALL THE WORLD DISSOLVES,
AND EVERY CREATURE SHALL BE PURIFIED,
ALL PLACES SHALL BE HELL THAT IS NOT HEAVEN.
                                        Christopher Marlowe
Nothing burns in Hell but the Self.
                                        St. Catherine of Genoa
    And when he was demanded of the Pharisees, when the kingdom of God should come, he answered them and said, The Kingdom of God cometh not with observation:
    Neither shall they say, Lo here! or, lo there! for, behold, the kingdom of God is within you.
                                        Luke, XVII, 20-21.

Unless you can find Heaven—within you—you remain in Hell, where burns the Self. In the twelve variations in this book, the twelve stories united only by the theme, the characters come increasingly closer to finding God within them. In the first story, a sandwich man, former banker, has a chance to begin again, but confronted with what he had run away from in the first place, he goes mad. In the second, a girl whose father destroyed love in her home runs away and becomes the next thing to a prostitute, a cadger of drinks from men, teasing them but not sleeping with them. When she realizes what she is, she goads a man to her destruction. In the third, a prim and sour woman, confronted with love, goes mad. In the fourth, completing the set, a husband and wife nag each other into destructive violence that ends in the outlet of sex. "The Red Sea" makes a kind of intermezzo, a fantasy about a Moses and a man who saw an illusion "and kept on drinking." Six is about a married couple who realize they have reached a dead end, and separate to try again. Seven is about a liberal of very high standards, who goes down in the world rather than compromise in any respect, but stands idly by, impotent, when violence strikes the one man who respected him. Eight is about spinster sisters, potentially lesbians, who, when the normal sex experience of one threatens to separate them, jump into the sea.

These two sets show a progress. In the first, the characters were so lost that when they caught merely a glimpse of themselves they had to turn to violence, death and madness—and the copulating couple show that there is more than one kind of madness, more than one kind of burning of the self. The second group are in sight of the promised land but cannot get there. The married couple in six go the wrong direction; the liberal sticks to the method that has cut away his effectiveness; the spinsters refuse to move at all.

In nine a disillusioned man becames a hermit—tries to escape from the world. He befriends a cat, and the cat's presence makes him see himself—and that the thing he was trying to escape was himself. In fury at his disillusionment he kills the cat, but then sentences himself to the purgatory of a menial job in a bank, where he will constantly be confronted with the thing he hates in himself. In ten, a sea captain, disinterested in his infant child, loving his wife, returns from a voyage to learn that his wife is dead. The child, he finds, is an idiot—but he still dedicates his life to it. In eleven, a well-to-do family, somehow in coming "up in the world" lost love. As a punishment for them, the father ruins them financially; then when he discovers that love is not lost, he begins again. "Victory," the last variation, already described, is a similar sacrifice, acted out to its conclusion. These people come close, but it is only in a kind of death that they find life, in a kind of Hell that they get some perception of Heaven.

The keys to this very unusual novel are in the theme story, the intermezzo, and the Prelude. In a way, *Not Heaven* is the Bible, transmuted by the interpretation Waldo Frank has made and is making of what should follow the Judeo-Christian culture; and translated into modern times. The Theme is the apocalypse; "The Red Sea" is the passage led by Moses, as the title clearly indicates, although the Children of Israel are slaves on an island plantation who were not freed at the end of the Civil War because the good news was withheld from them. The Prelude, "Antient History," is something of an Iliad to the Bible as Odyssey; it shows man in a garden of Eden but unhappy there because of his sophistication.

We move into the main part of "Antient History" by means of the satiric story of J. V. Bonabath, who painted pictures in his garret in Illyria, Ohio, until he was satisfied with them, then offered them to an art dealer, who arranged an exhibition and exploited every opportunity to make them popular. They were popular; they showed simple, everyday scenes, but none of the figures were clothed. They made such a success that clothing was banned all over the world, and the technology that had been dedicated to weapons was turned to creating heating plants, to make the climate temperate through the year all over the earth.

Thus comes the main part of the story. Man is returned to Eden—or progressed to Utopia, as you prefer. The vanities of the world disappear; jewelry, armies, the priesthood of both the church and the school, and the machinery man sets up between himself and nature do not harmonize with man out of clothes. But boredom sets in. This boredom, breaking out in all sorts of outrages, is temporarily stemmed by a prophet who teaches that God is within each person, and that worship of God is awareness of the God within. The interpreters, after the prophet has died, raise controversies that gradually bring back the old faults, and with them come clothes again.

The regions were nations again, manufacturing clothes and patriotism, preserving their atomic and solar resources for defense. The day came when an open war was declared—between the South African Union and Brazil. The dispute was over the possession of a newly discovered island near Tristan da Cunha in the Atlantic. It was a mere splinter of rock, uninhabited except by marine birds whose guano was precious for the extraction of solar energy. In the first hour of hostilities, all the large cities of both nations were destroyed from the air, and a chance bomb (no one knew whether African or Brazilian) wiped out the tiny guano island. The survivors of both nations—now without cities and without an island to fight for—vowed they would struggle to the end. The world breathed a sigh of satisfaction,—somewhat like a man after a hot day's work who sinks into the armchair on the porch, while some one hands him a cool drink. Tomorrow, dammit, will be another day; but for the moment, he forgets. . . .

This story is very many things. It is, for one, an anti-utopia; a statement like *Brave New World*, *Limbo*, and other such novels, that man will not achieve a satisfactory life through changes in the externals. As an anti-utopia, "Antient History" goes farther than any of the others, presenting the most satisfactory utopia in demonstrating that the idea of utopia is a false one. But in addition, the story is an application of the histories of the Bible to today's technology; indeed, with its savior in the form of the prophet, it is a history of civilization, that from barbarism went to paganism, and was transformed by Christianity only to have strife within Christianity produce the germs that destroy its effect. The message of the prophet, however, is not the part of Christ's sayings that is usually emphasized; it is rather that part of them which Waldo Frank has emphasized. It is as if he were saying: Even if this book produces as much effect as the Bible—even if I be considered a prophet—there is a danger of misusing what I have taught. Each man must actively find God for himself.

Following the prelude, the stories tell first of those who found only Hell, then, after "The Red Sea," of those admitted to Purgatory. "The Red Sea," one of the strangest and most fascinating stories in the book, serves to point up the unity between the Person and the People; the slaves, kept in bondage after the Civil War, freeing themselves, are symbolic of the coming of age of the colored races.

In the Theme, "The Kingdom of Heaven," a person passes through Purgatory and gets a glimpse of Heaven. He is an Argentinian revolutionist, a poet, who, captured by his enemies, is sewed in the skin of a freshly-killed steer and left to die in the sun of the pampa. In the excruciating torture he gains clarity about the unity of all things—his childhood, the vultures, the ants, the *caudillo* who put him there.

> The earth and the sun of ecstasy vanished, only the thirst and the fire remaining. He saw, directly before him, the *caudillo*. He was a bearded vulture with the vulture's eyes and the smile on his

hard mouth making it a beak. His shirt and brown *bombachas* had the shape of folded wings.

"What is this God of yours?" asked the red eyes. "He gives you nerves to torture you; pride to humiliate you; dreams and a heart in order to break them; life in order to kill. . . . A clever cruel son-of-bitch, your God. Don't contradict me."

"I don't."

"So you agree?"

"That's your part of the truth. Fly away and wait for it."

Thus far we have no more than is in the Book of Job. The concluding paragraph seems to go a bit beyond it:

Juan saw himself standing naked and alone in the pampa. His limbs could not hold him; he stood because he was suspended in the tension of two poles: one, huge, parabolic, the world unto the stars; one, dimensionless, within him. Juan's legs folded, his body sank to the earth and lay prostrate. The ants marched, the vultures with raw cry circled down. But he stood. He lay on his back, and his eyes saw the eyes of the vultures. He stood. . . .

It is not that, having gone through martyrdom, Juan was admitted to Heaven, but that his vision under torture was such that he could see the kingdom of Heaven within him.

Not Heaven is the culmination of what Frank had been striving for up to this time. Like *City Block*, that in its time presented Frank's philosophy of the Person transformed by an awareness of the Cosmos with its human relationships similarly based on sound psychology, and its most incidental characters three-dimensional and well motivated, in a form created for the purpose, and with symbolism as many-layered as a poem, it presents, through Persons, the concept of the Person and the People, identically aware of the Cosmos. The unity around the theme, with a prelude and variations of those who do not achieve Heaven, and the theme and intermezzo of a person and a people who do, is not the only unity of the novel, any more than the fact that they all lived on the same block made the unity in *City Block*. It is rather that in Waldo Frank's philosophy, there is no such thing as an individual: persons exist only in relation to all the other things in the universe; and the unity which is all creation is God. As he says in his "Aside to the Reader," ". . . deeper than this surface unity of scene [in *City Block*] is the attempted unity of each episode's passional crisis, which joins the characters beyond the separate cells of their lives, and merges them upon a common Ground of consciousness and revelation." His aim, he says, is "to reveal the relationship of persons beyond the carnal and fortuitous: their relationship, in a given time and land where they are strangers, to the eternal Ground, active within them, whose dimensions both within and beyond time-space inevitably *locate* the characters by different coordinates than the flat ones of conventional fiction."

For *Ground* read *God*, not describable by noun, but by verb: I am that I am. The thing we have in common is the truth of our life and all the heaven we could wish for; and in our awareness of self is our awareness of God. To explain in denotative language what Waldo Frank thus far has explained only by use of highly developed symbols goes beyond the scope of the critic; Frank himself is now engaged in completing a statement of all this, a book to be called *The Rediscovery of Man*. The perceptive reader will probably still, when that is written, be able to find facets of meaning in *Not Heaven* that are not covered in the book to come; there are things in *City Block* that go far beyond the explanations of *The Re-Discovery of America*.

It is a constant growth, a constant application to new problems, achieved through his fiction and explained in part by his cultural study that is the main characteristic of Waldo Frank the man and the artist. His philosophy seems to have been developed chiefly through his fiction, which in turn is explanation of and experiment with his development as a person. Whatever failures may be found in his novels are failures in himself, failures to achieve himself as a person; as he continues to develop as a person, new developments in his fiction can be expected.

After the publication of Not Heaven early in 1953, Frank turned to preparing The Rediscovery of Man, the definitive statement of his philosophy. As when he was preparing Re-Discovery and Chart, he began producing more and more political and critical journalism, ranging from studies of Whitman and Thoreau to the extensive Nation article, "Toward a New Radicalism." Among other things, he accepted the assignment to write a syndicated column, "Voz de América," for distribution in Latin America. When his book was in first draft, he visited Israel, planning to do a series of articles on the Jewish state for "Voz." The series, as well might be expected, turned out to be a book, Bridgehead.

Although books on Israel have been notoriously poor sellers, and nearly every one of the magazines directed at a mainly Jewish readership reviewed it very adversely, Bridgehead has enjoyed an unusual success. This seemed to be one book on Israel that appealed, not because the readers were emotionally involved in the subject, but for the sake of its intrinsic worth. For the first time Frank was reaching a wide audience on the merits of his vision and writing alone.

The theme of the book is simply Frank's concept of the Person, the People, and the Whole applied to a particular situation. He finds Israel a bridgehead of the West in the Middle East, and warns that Jews must make themselves worthy— through following their traditional obligation of the Covenant— to help the Arabs overcome the oppression of their masters and the exploitation of colonialism. The greatest shortcoming of the book is political; since Frank's active concern with politics, in the thirties, the creative power of nationalism as well as its vulnerability to demagoguery has been greatly intensified. But

Frank is confused by the Sabras, who know Israel as home, not as refuge, and he fails to discuss the spirit of creative nationalism.

Nevertheless, *Bridgehead* brought him back into the public eye. *The Rediscovery of Man*, discussion of which is far beyond the scope of this study, will appear in 1958. Then, if the past is any indication, Frank will return to the novel. For all his long quest and steady progress, he still has several problems to solve in his fiction. Most important of these is, once a character has achieved Person-hood, what is he to do? David Markand and Mary Donald set out to live in terms of love, but what action can they perform in a world of hate? The poet in *Not Heaven* sees the heaven within him as he dies, but can one not see it and live? Can the action of the Person be dramatic?

Another area Frank has brushed past in his novels is man in the face of inexorable violence: war, brutal totalitarianism, thought-control and brainwashing. He knows and has written of all these things, but not in fiction. The battle of the person against dogmatic authority has been the subject of a good many satiric novels, from *The Good Soldier Schweik* to the current crop of "hipster" novels; but can the subject be treated both seriously and creatively?

Above all else, he needs to refine his vocabulary. Hemingway and Eliot *have* had a contribution to make. Joyce and Nathanael West have made prose fiction as sensitive as poetry. Frank has contributed a superb theme and *Weltanschauung;* his technique of characterization has carried us beyond the primitive concepts our ancestors stopped at; but his efforts are hampered by occasional obsolete and pretentious use of words. With this he is in good company: Poe, to mention a master who often transcended this flaw, with it blemished his most profound works. Like Poe, too, Frank writes as he does because his artistic qualities are often in competition with a keen analytical reasoning power.

The tragedy of Poe was that the older he grew, the less able he was to curb his rational mind's interference with his unconscious creativity. Not so with Frank. *Not Heaven*, the nearly automatic result of an urge to dig up a few themes for stories to be sold to the magazines, is his finest creative effort, rivalled only by the similarly-organized lyric novels of the twenties. Like all writers, Frank's best work emerged where his feelings overpowered his calculated plan; in his longer novels this happened when he was inspired by the world of his second wife *(The Bridegroom Cometh)* or of his father *(Island in the Atlantic)*; but in *The Death and Birth of David Markand* the idea stifles the art.

No matter what judgment posterity makes on the fictional works of Waldo Frank, it seems hardly likely that he will not be considered a great originator in the novel. He has freed prose fiction, at the time it needs it most, of the limitations of a mythology that made its highest literary form tragedy and held its attitude toward humanity to the psychology of ancient Greece. He is a philosopher so creative that he had to use an art form—the novel—to express his vision; and when he found that form inadequate to his purpose, created a new form to suit his new conception. His cultural contribution has not been questioned; this, without doubt, makes his esthetic contribution of equal value or, if writers in the future use it wisely, of infinitely greater value.

Selected Bibliography

A COMPLETE BIBLIOGRAPHY OF THE ARTICLES, TRANSLATIONS, AND reprints of Waldo Frank's books would be much too long to be included here. A bibliography of Frank's works in the English language, prepared by Jerome Kloucek at Northwestern University, occupies more pages than does this entire study. I therefore have listed only the first editions of Frank's books, and books that have been exclusively concerned with him.

NOVELS

The Unwelcome Man. Boston: Little, Brown and Company, 1917.
The Dark Mother. New York: Boni and Liveright, 1920.
City Block. Darien, Conn.: Waldo Frank, 1922. (Limited edition of 1,250 copies.)
Rahab. New York: Boni and Liveright, 1922.
Holiday. New York: Boni and Liveright, 1924.
Chalk Face. New York: Boni and Liveright, 1925.
The Death and Birth of David Markand. New York: Charles Scribner's Sons, 1934.
The Bridegroom Cometh. New York: Doubleday, Doran and Company, 1939. (First publication, London, Gollancz, 1938.)
Summer Never Ends. New York: Duell, Sloane and Pearce, 1940.
Island in the Atlantic. New York: Duell, Sloan and Pearce, 1946.
The Invaders. New York: Duell, Sloan and Pearce, 1948.
Not Heaven. New York: Hermitage House, 1953.

CULTURAL CRITICISM

Our America. New York: Boni and Liveright, 1919.
Virgin Spain. New York: Boni and Liveright, 1926.

Re-Discovery of America. New York: Charles Scribner's Sons, 1929.
America Hispana. New York: Charles Scribner's Sons, 1931.
Dawn in Russia. New York: Charles Scribner's Sons, 1932.
In the American Jungle. New York: Farrar and Rinehart, 1937.
Chart for Rough Water. New York: Doubleday, Doran and Company, 1940.
South American Journey. New York: Duell, Sloan and Pearce, 1943.
The Jew in Our Day. New York: Duell, Sloan and Pearce, 1944.
Birth of a World. Boston: Houghton Mifflin Company, 1951.
Bridgehead. New York: George Braziller, Inc., 1957.
The Rediscovery of Man. New York: George Braziller, Inc., 1958.

LITERARY CRITICISM

Art of the Vieux Colombier. Paris: Nouvelle Revue Française, 1917.
Salvos. New York: Boni and Liveright, 1926. (Includes Art of the Vieux Colombier.)
Time Exposures (By Search-Light). New York: Boni and Liveright, 1927.

WORKS PUBLISHED ONLY IN SPANISH

Primer Mensaje á la América Hispana. Madrid: Revista de Occidente, 1930.
Ustedes y Nosotros. Buenos Aires: Losada, 1942.

CRITICISM

Munson, Gorham. Waldo Frank: A Study. New York: Boni and Liveright, 1923.
Benardete, M. J. (ed.). Waldo Frank in America Hispana. New York: Instituto de las Españas en los Estados Unidos, Columbia University, 1929.

Index

Date Due

AG 1 62			

Demco 293-5